William Wolfe Capes

University Life in Ancient Athens

Being the substance of four Oxford lectures

William Wolfe Capes

University Life in Ancient Athens
Being the substance of four Oxford lectures

ISBN/EAN: 9783337035990

Printed in Europe, USA, Canada, Australia, Japan

Cover: Foto ©ninafisch / pixelio.de

More available books at **www.hansebooks.com**

UNIVERSITY LIFE IN ANCIENT ATHENS

BEING THE SUBSTANCE OF FOUR OXFORD LECTURES

BY

W. W. CAPES, M.A.

READER IN ANCIENT HISTORY IN THE UNIVERSITY OF OXFORD

LONDON
LONGMANS, GREEN, AND CO.
1877

All rights reserved

PREFACE.

THESE PAGES have been written simply as a chapter in the history of the past, which is little known perhaps among us. Modern names and analogies have been freely used, but only to assist the fancy, and with no wish to imply, by way of oblique reference, any judgment on the merits or demerits of our present system. Comparison may possibly be useful, but the reader is asked to draw his conclusions for himself, and not to ascribe them to the writer. The materials for the first chapter are gathered almost exclusively from monumental sources, which may be most easily consulted in a work by A. Dumont 'Sur l'Éphébie Attique,' of which one volume only, containing the Greek texts, had appeared before these sheets were printed.

The early part of the second chapter is based on an article by C. G. Zumpt on the Schools of Philosophy at Athens, which was published in 1843, in the Transactions of the Academy of Berlin, but the original authorities have been throughout consulted. In the other pages frequent references have been made to the biographies by Philostratus and Eunapius, who deal especially with the subjects treated. The writings of Libanius have been also largely used, though his pictures of professorial and student life are only partly drawn from Athens, which he left to lecture at Antioch and elsewhere, but there is no reason to believe that his descriptions do not apply to the conditions of the older University. For an introduction to the lectures of Himerius, the writer was indebted to a treatise by L. Petit de Julleville, 'L'École d'Athènes au quatrième Siècle,' as also possibly for one or two other hints. Hertzberg's 'Geschichte Griechenlands unter der Herrschaft der Römer' has also been consulted, as containing probably the fullest treatment of the subject, but from that source little or nothing in the following pages has been consciously derived.

BRAMSHOTT: *March* 1877.

CONTENTS.

INTRODUCTION 1–3
                                             PAGE.

CHAPTER I.

THE COLLEGE SYSTEM.

Our information comes from the inscriptions of the Ephebi which extend for centuries 4
Early usages with regard to the Ephebi 5
Important changes in the Macedonian period 6
Many Athenians never were included 6
Aliens were admitted 6
The Term was shortened 7
Matriculation and religious ceremony at the opening of Term 7
Stress laid on religious influence, and holy seasons . . 8
Their academic dress 9
They probably lived together 10
Their use of gymnasia 10
They attended the Lectures of the Public Professors . . 12
Attendance at all except the Epicurean, encouraged . . 12
The term of College life was very short 13
But the expenses considerable. College dues . . . 14
Payment to College Library 14
Offertory. Testimonials. Athletic Sports. Sconces . . 15
The final examinations in the Senate House . . . 16
Their healthy state and good behaviour 17
The Cosmetes or Head of the College 18

Contents.

	PAGE
The Sophronistæ or Proctors. Tutors. College Accounts	19
The vote of thanks in the Public Assembly	20
A characteristic specimen recorded in the inscriptions	21
The System above described was a national one	25
Our information drawn almost entirely from the inscriptions	26
These give the number and names of the students, many of whom were Semitic	27

CHAPTER II.

The Professors of Philosophy.

The four great schools of thought	29
The succession in each school religiously respected	30
The heads lectured in the public gymnasia	31
Rudimentary forms of endowment in the Platonic sect	32
,, ,, ,, in the Aristotelian	33
,, ,, ,, in the Epicurean	34
Endowments for philosophic dinners, which tended to become extravagant	35
No legal recognition of corporate rights in the sects	37
They resented any interference from the State	38
Fees paid by the students	39
The Cynic or Stoic sect discouraged endowments and fees	39
The large number of students of philosophy	40
Stories of sudden conversion	41
Honorary recognition of the philosophers by Athens	41
Little endowment as yet needed	42
Rival seats of learning for other branches of study	42
The influence of old associations in favour of Athens	43
Yet her attractive power grew weaker	44
Her revival thanks to the patronage of Hadrian, and the Antonines, who began the system of State endowments	45
Lucian's description of an Election by a Board	46
A more favourable picture of Athenian society by the same author	47
Also in Aulus Gellius	48
The description of Herodes Atticus	50
Few signs of originality or deep study in later days	51

CHAPTER III.

THE PROFESSORS OF RHETORIC.

	PAGE
The Sophists or Professors of Rhetoric	53
The public professors and private lecturers generally aliens, often men of wealth and rank	54
The story of Hippodromus to illustrate the knight errantry of the Sophists	56
The story of Marcus of Byzantium	57
Popular enthusiasm for the Sophists. Their vanity and ostentation	58
Their professional gains	60
Their immunities from civil burdens	61
Examples of imperial caprice in the treatment of the Sophists	62
The interests of learning suffered from the whims of Caracalla	63
And in the third century from war and faction . . .	64
Athens stormed by the Goths, who were routed by Dexippus	65
The fourth century a brilliant age for the University of Athens	65
The endowed Chairs, and influence of the Provincial Governor	67
Official salaries varying like tithe rent charge. Lecture-rooms	68
Jealousies of rival Sophists illustrated from Eunapius . .	69
Another illustration of their bitter feeling and rhetorical skill	71
The three great Sophists rather Asiatic than Hellenic in race	73
The general character of their educational influence . .	74
The personal ties between teacher and student were very close, and desertion keenly felt by the lecturer . .	75
The evils of rivalry sometimes avoided by special unions .	76
The position of the sub-professors in these is not attractive	77
Libanius called to account for neglect of professorial work	78
The Sophists' pride in the number of their pupils . .	79
The solemn language of Himerius to the freshmen . .	80
The course consisted of the study of the Classics, together with the rules of rhetoric	81
Original compositions were required, and exercises in logic and elocution	83

	PAGE
The Sophists professed to aim at more than rhetoric	84
But the course of study was more imposing than profound	85
The evidence remaining in the works of Professors like Himerius	86
The difficulty of doing justice to the rhetorical beauties of Greek style	87
Themistius, though a philosopher, is as rhetorical as the Sophists	89
As moral preachers the Sophists were surpassed by Christian doctors	90
The dwindling numbers and reputation of the Schools	91
Illustrations from Libanius of the poverty of Professors	93

CHAPTER IV.

STUDENT LIFE.

Our knowledge mainly drawn from writers of the fourth century	96
Few students were of Attic race	96
Commonly they were very young and had pedagogues often	97
Each attached himself specially to a Professor	98
The students touting for their own Professors.—Experience of Libanius	99
The practical jokes which few freshmen escaped	100
National differences seem to have been marked by social clubs	102
The factious spirit of these illustrated by Eunapius	103
Effect of such students' brawls on the fancy of the young Libanius	105
Town and gown riots	106
Attacks upon the pedagogues	107
No discipline exerted by the University or by city police	108
Very different provisions at Rome	109
The students at Lecture	110
They often behaved badly, as Libanius describes	111
Even in earlier ages there is evidence of rudeness and inattention	113
Question among the Sophists as to the use of the rod	114

Contents. xi

PAGE

Himerius relied on love, but Libanius used the rod, though
    he shrank from expulsion 115
Students often would not pay the fees 116
Many of them were very poor, and there were no exhibitions 118
They often remained long, and left the University with
    regret 119

CHAPTER V.

CHRISTIAN INFLUENCES ON THE SCHOOLS OF ATHENS.

The early Sophists were freethinkers, the later conservative
    in religion 120
The later philosophers were devout and claimed powers over
    the spirit world 121
The Christian alarm and dislike of the schools of rhetoric . 122
The complaints of Libanius of the discouragement to study 123
Brighter times came in with Julian, but were not lasting . 124
His death was followed by edicts and riots against Paganism 126
The bitter resentment of Eunapius and Libanius . . . 127
The schools of Athens suffered from the downfall of Paganism, and from the spread of legal and Latin studies . . 129
Synesius tells us of pilgrims attracted to Athens . . . 130
But he speaks with contempt of the studies carried on there 131
The schools of rhetoric disappeared 132
These were closed by the edict of Justinian . . . 133
A few philosophers retired to Persia, but only to be disappointed of their hopes 134

CHRONOLOGICAL TABLE.

	B.C.
The death of Socrates	399
Plato in the Academy	388
Antisthenes the Cynic	*fl.* 366
Speusippus, Head of the Academy	347–339
Xenocrates succeeded Speusippus	339
Isocrates wrote the Panegyr. 380	*died* † 338
Aristotle in the Lyceum	335
Crates the Cynic	*fl.* 328
Theophrastus succeeded Aristotle in the Lyceum	322
Demetrius Phalereus, Governor of Athens	318
Polemon succeeded Xenocrates	315
Epicurus at Athens	306
Straton succeeded Theophrastus	*about* 287
Antigonus Gonatas	283–239
Zenon in the Porch	*fl.* 278
Lycon succeeded Straton	272
Cleanthes succeeded Zenon	263
Chrysippus succeeded Cleanthes	*born* 280 † 207
Carneades, Ambassador of Athens	155
Siege of Athens by Sulla	87
Cicero at Athens	79
Horace at the University	47
	A.D.
Athens declined in reputation	
Dion Chrysostom	*fl. about* 97
Epictetus	*fl.* ,, 104
Plutarch	*fl.* ,, 115

Chronological Table.

	A.D.
Hadrian beautified Athens	124
The Sophists, Favorinus and Polemon . . . *fl.*	132
Herodes Atticus, 101-177 . . . . . *consul*	143
Aulus Gellius at Athens	160-4
Marcus Aurelius, Emperor } The University endowed }	161-180
Lucian wrote . . . . . . *fl. about*	162
Aristides wrote his sermons	175
The Deipnosophistæ of Athenæus written	193
Philostratus wrote the lives of the Sophists . *after*	221
Plotinus	205-270
Diogenes Laertius . . . . . *fl. about*	250
Dexippus routed the Goths	269
Longinus . . . . †	273
Eumenius 'pro restaurandis scholis'	296
Himerius	315-368
Libanius at Athens	336
Death of Julian the Sophist	340
Libanius, Professor at Antioch } Themistius, Professor at Constantinople }	352
Letter of Emperor Julian to people of Athens	361
Eunapius born 346 . . . . . at Athens	362
Death of Proæresius	367
Synesius at Athens . . . . . *about*	390
Death of Libanius	396
Eunapius wrote the lives of the Sophists . . *about*	406
Plutarch at Athens . . . . †	431
Justinian closed the Schools of Athens	529

UNIVERSITY LIFE IN ANCIENT ATHENS.

INTRODUCTION.

WHEN Pericles reminded his Athenian hearers, in his famous funeral speech, that their fatherland was a sort of school of Greece, he was using words unconsciously that were weighty with prophetic meaning. He was thinking of the monumental glories of the city, which strangers flocked from every land to visit; of the impulse given to art-studies by the genius of Phidias, and of his band of fellow-labourers on the Acropolis; of the outburst of literary talent stirred by the strong sense of national freedom; of the charms of poetry and music enlisted in the service of the stately ceremonials of religion. But the professional teachers of his day were aliens for the most part; Sophists, cosmopolitan in feeling, who settled in the Imperial city because they found there a ready mart for all their foreign wares, where practised skill in fence of words was needed most

Thuc. ii. 41.

for the free play of national life. In the orator's own days, however, the movement was beginning which was to render Athens before long the home of intellectual training. Socrates was dropping into the minds of his young friends those fruitful seeds which, modified by the various soils on which they fell, were to grow in course of time into the four great schools of thought, which between them occupied well-nigh all earnest seekers after truth. They quartered themselves in Athens as their home, assuming each an organised shape, and gathering admirers from all lands.

Around them was grouped a multitude of other teachers, lecturers in rhetoric and grammar, who dressed up in popular and showy forms their theories of literary art. And so men came to think of her as the University of higher culture, in which were represented all the studies of the age.

The Ethical systems took to some extent, as Bacon says, the place which Theology has filled elsewhere, while the ancient Metaphysic dealt more expressly with many of her problems. Physical enquiry of a kind was encouraged in the Lyceum, as a part of the encyclopædia of Aristotle. Logical method was pursued, though on different principles, by all; and the Rhetoricians, too, were busy supplying something like courses of philology, or the ' Literæ

Humaniores' of our later times. Private benefactors before long came forward with endowments to provide a quiet shelter for the chief professors of each school, the local permanence of which was thus secured. Soon, indeed, Athens had to stoop from her former rank among the nations; but she stepped almost at once into another, and became the school. not of Greece only, but the world.

After a while again she suffered from the rivalry of other intellectual centres, as also from the marked decline of original research. But the endowments of the Antonines gave her a new lease of life, and in the third and fourth centuries she was, beyond compare, the foremost of the Universities then known.

She lingered on a century longer, though in spectral form and with decaying strength, till the edict of Justinian closed her schools; and her professors moodily withdrew to far-off Persia, to seek, though vainly, for the enlightened favour which was denied them in the Roman Empire.

A.D. 529.

CHAPTER I.

THE COLLEGE SYSTEM.

Our information comes from the inscriptions of the Ephebi,

SOME scholars may be inclined to call in question the term which has been chosen for the heading of this chapter; may doubt if there was anything at Athens which could answer to the College Life of modern times. Indeed it must be owned that formal history is nearly silent on the subject, that ancient writers take little notice of it, and such evidences as we have are drawn almost entirely from a series of inscriptions on the marble tablets, which were covered with the ruins and the dust of ages, till one after another came to light in recent days, to add fresh pages to the story of the past.

which extend for centuries.

Happily they are both numerous and lengthy, and may be already pieced together in an order which extends for centuries. They are known to Epigraphic students as the records which deal with the so-called *Ephebi*; with the youths, that is, just passing into manhood, for whom a special discipline was provided by the State, to fit them for the responsibilities of active life. It was a National system with a many-sided training; the teachers were members of the Civil Service; the registers were public documents, and, as such, belonged to the Archives of the State. The earlier inscriptions of the series date from the period of Macedonian ascendency, but in much earlier times there had been forms of public drill prescribed for the Ephebi. It had been an ancient usage that the youths who had just entered on their nineteenth year should appear, in the presence of their kinsfolk and their neighbours, to have their names put on the Civic Roll, to be armed in public with a shield and spear, and to be then escorted to a temple where the solemn oath was taken of loyal service to their country and their gods. 'I swear,' so ran the words, 'not to bring disgrace upon these arms, nor to desert my comrade in the fight. I will do battle for the common weal, for the religion of my fathers. I will obey those who bear rule, and the laws which are in force, and all that the sovereign people shall decree.' The young champions so pledged were bound awhile to special forms of military duty; they were drafted into companies of National guards, and patrolled the country districts, or were posted in outlying forts in defensive service on the frontier, till their two years of probation had expired.

Early usages with regard to the Ephebi.

Such were the forms which lasted on through the old days of independence, when every citizen must be a soldier, and the first claim which Athens made was that her children should defend her. But in the later days of Macedonian rule, when she enjoyed only a faint show of freedom, she no longer demanded as a right the personal service of her sons, and soon changed, in the case of the Ephebi, the essential character of her educational routine.

Important changes in the Macedonian period.

1. The name did not henceforth include the whole rising manhood of the State. All who feared the loss of time or want of means, all who thought the drill too irksome, could stand aside when they reached the fitting age, and not enrol themselves in what was now a corps of Volunteers. The poorer classes, as we may suppose, dropped out, and betook themselves at once to active life; only the well-to-do aspired to such a finish to a liberal training.

Many Athenians never were included.

2. It served no longer as a test of purity of birth or civic rights. We find from a decree, which, if genuine, dates even from the days of Pericles, that the young men of Cos were allowed by special favour to share the discipline of the Athenian Ephebi. Soon afterwards others were admitted on all sides. The aliens who had gained a competence as merchants or as bankers, found their sons welcomed in the ranks of the oldest families of Athens; strangers flocked thither from dis-

Aliens were admitted.

tant countries, not only from the isles of Greece, and from the coasts of the Ægean, but, as Hellenic culture made its way through the far East, students even of Semitic race were glad to enrol their names upon the College registers, where we may still see them with the marks of their several nationalities affixed.

3. The young men were no longer, like soldiers upon actual service, beginning already the real work of life, and on that account, perhaps, the term was shortened from two years to one; but the old associations lasted on for ages, even in realistic Athens, which in early politics at least had made so clean a sweep. The outward forms were still preserved, the soldier's drill was still enforced, and, though many another feature had been added, the whole institution bore upon its face the look rather of a Military College than of a training school for a scholar or a statesman. *The term was shortened.*

The College year began somewhat later than the opening of the civil year, and it was usual for all the students to matriculate together; that is, to enter formally their names upon the registers, which were copied afterwards upon the marble tablets, of which large fragments have survived. That done, they were expected to take part, with their officers and tutors, in a religious ceremonial held in the Guild- *Matriculation, and religious ceremony at the opening of Term;*

hall of the city, which even in its name reminds us of our stated services at the opening of Term.

For the Athenian Government laid special stress upon religious influence in education; they insisted that the young men should be trained to reverence the guardian powers of the State. The documents before us emphasize the hope that they would grow to orderly and pious manhood; and, with all their large tolerance of Nonconformist systems, the rulers had no scruple in prescribing the religion of the State. The creeds of Paganism were too wide and too elastic to cause anxiety to any tender conscience, and the votaries of Syrian gods could join without misgiving in the ritual of Hellenic worship. Even to the last days of the heathen world, Athens was the stronghold of religious feeling. Old associations lingered round its venerable walls, and linked themselves to great historic names, as in our modern Oxford, till those even owned the glamour of the ancient city, whose reason had rebelled against its outworn dogmas. We may read, therefore, of a long round of special times, like the holy seasons and the saints' days of our modern calendars, which were all of interest to the young men at College, not as holidays from earnest work, but as days of ceremonial observance. At some they walked in military guise, like Hungarian students at the Stephan's fest, march-

for stress was laid on religious influence in education,

and many holy seasons were observed.

ing through the streets of Pesth with their swords buckled to their sides; at some they moved in slow procession with their lighted torches, like an Academic club of Germany; at other times they joined in a thanksgiving service or State prayers for a victory won centuries before, like that of Marathon, engaging in mimic contests to revive the excitement of the past; while, in honour of the triumphs won upon the sea at Salamis, they raced over the waters, and made processions with their boats, as in later ages on the Isis or the Cam. In most of these, as on other State occasions, they wore the same official dress which distinguished them from all beside. 'To put the gown on,' or, as we should say, 'to be a gownsman,' was the phrase which stood for being a member of the College; and the gown, too, was of black, as commonly among ourselves. *Their academic dress.*

But Philostratus tells us, by the way, that a change was made from black to white at the prompting of Herodes Atticus, the munificent and learned subject of the Antonines, who was for many years the presiding genius of the University of Athens. The fragment of an inscription lately found curiously confirms and supplements the writer's statement. Herodes, it would seem, did not only introduce the more auspicious colour, but defrayed himself the expenses of the charge, and is represented in the *Philostratus, ii. 59, ed. Trübner.*

contemporary document as saying, 'While I am living you shall never want white robes.' Some may possibly remember the attempt made nearly twenty years ago to introduce a seemlier form of gown for use among the Commoners of Oxford; but no Herodes Oxoniensis volunteered to meet the objection of expense, and so make the change easier for slender purses.

They probably lived ogether.

The members of the College are spoken of as 'friends' and 'messmates;' and it is probable that some form of conventual life prevailed among them, without which the drill and supervision, which are constantly implied in the inscriptions, could scarcely have been enforced by the officials. But we know nothing of any public buildings for their use save the *gymnasia*, which in all Greek towns were the centres of educational routine, and of which there were several well known at Athens. Drawing, as they did, their name from the bodily exercises for which they had been first provided, and serving in this respect for men as well as boys, they were used also for the culture of the mind. Public lecturers of every kind resorted to them, philosophy sought to gain a hearing in their halls, and rival systems even took their names from buildings such as these, where they catered for the intellect, while trainers a few yards off were drilling the body in the laws of healthy work. One such especi-

Their use of the gymnasia for various sides of educational training.

ally, the Diogeneum, served as a centre of stirring College life; the President, who had the charge of it, is one of the officials often mentioned. Here probably they had a College library, as also certainly in another called the Ptolemæum. In such gymnasia a variety of trainers were employed to call out the physical powers in the full energy of balanced life. Here the youths qualified themselves as marksmen in the use of the javelin and the bow, and a separate instructor was appointed in each case. Here, too, they were practised in the drill which was to fit them for their Grand Parades, at which the public would look on, and the Chief Minister of State preside. Athletic sports of every kind found in such scenes a natural home. They were encouraged, almost prescribed in this case, by the government, which showed a lively interest in what was done. Here, too, the students fell into their ranks as Volunteers, and marched out to form an escort for some distinguished stranger who favoured Athens with a visit. Or they formed themselves into a guard of honour, and kept order in the sittings of the National Assemblies, listening meantime to the course of the debates, and gaining betimes an insight into the business of public life, and a personal acquaintance with the prominent statesmen of the day. But they had their livelier spectacles at times. They went to the theatre to see the play together, and there they had, we read, their proper places kept for them in a sort of Undergraduates' Gallery.

They had to attend lectures;

They had their lectures also to attend, in their own gymnasia or in other buildings of the kind; for they were not allowed to slight the chances of intellectual progress in the eager love of races, sports, and volunteering. Some sort of certificate of attendance at the courses was seemingly required.

but at the courses of the public professors

But in this respect, at least, the College did not try to monopolise the education of its students. It had, indeed, its own tutors or instructors, but they were kept for humbler drill; it did not even for a long time keep an organist or choirmaster of its own; it sent its students out for teaching in philosophy and rhetoric and grammar, or, in a word, for all the larger and more liberal studies. Nor did it favour any special set of tenets to the exclusion of the rest. It

attendance was impartially encouraged,

encouraged impartially all the schools of higher thought. One document which we possess speaks approvingly of the young men's attendance in the lecture-hall of a Professor who expounded seemingly the Stoic system, but it goes on to note that they were present also at the courses given by Platonists and Aristotelians alike. The context even would imply that they went together in a body, attended by their Head, and listened to the lectures of all the Professors; or, as the inscriptions more than once record, of *all the philosophers* who taught their theories in public. The College had no fear, it seems, of critical enquiry and free thought, though it may, perhaps, have overtasked the receptive powers of its students. One only of the great historic systems was ignored, perhaps as likely to be pushed too far by inexperienced minds to some extreme of dangerous licence, or rank impatience of control. No mention is ever made of the theories of Epicurus, which were judged, probably, unfit for the youths who were still ' *in statu pupillari.*' The appetite for knowledge thus excited could be ill satisfied with a few months of lectures; but, though the discipline so far described lasted only for a year, there was nothing to prevent them from carrying on their interest in high thought. As students unattached they might linger for years round the same lecture-halls, busy themselves with the same unsolved problems, and in their turn hold conferences on great occasions, or aspire to fill some public Chair of Morals or Philology.

<small>except the Epicurean.</small>

The term, indeed, was far too short for such a multifarious training, which was at once gymnastic, martial, intellectual, and moral; but many even in those days were reluctant, it would seem, to postpone the active work of life in the interests of higher culture.

<small>The term of College life was very short,</small>

but the expenses considerable.

College dues.

Payment to College library.

As it is, the names of the old families figure most upon the registers; for there were other forms of outlay, besides the expenditure of valuable time, to deter the less opulent of the middle classes. We read nothing indeed of College dues, or of the sums paid for batells by the students; and more than once the authorities are praised in the inscriptions for lowering, if not remitting altogether, certain charges. It is possible that the expense was partly met by a grant of public money, or by some form of endowment; and the mention that recurs of the sacrifices in the memory of past benefactors seems to point to this conclusion, while it reminds us of the Bidding Prayer in which we hear the names of the pious founders of old time. But of the accounts, which were to be audited each year in public by some officials of the State, it is most likely that the payments of the young men themselves formed an important item.

Nor did their expenses end with those for board or for tuition. Each must pay his quota to provide a hundred volumes yearly for the College library, which was stored, as we have seen, in a gymnasium. Their piety must be attested by liberal offerings to the Mother of the Gods and Dionysus, and sometimes, too, to other powers. Nor was it left to them to give at their free will; but a decree is quoted which defined the amount to be expended, somewhat

as a few years back at Oxford the Chapel offertory   Offertory.
was charged in College batells. Each generation
left behind it year by year the pieces of gold and
silver plate which, duly emblazoned doubtless with
their names, were stored up—not in the College
buttery, but in the treasury of some temple.
Four costly goblets of the kind, we read in one inscription, were presented by the students of a single
year.

The Rectors, too, who did their duty, must re-   Testi-
ceive some sort of testimonial, and have their bronze   monials.
or marble statues presented to them by their grateful
pupils, as men accept their pictures nowadays. It
became at last a customary thing, to be mentioned
in the record of each year; and therefore the honour
was but trifling, though the cost was real, and the
omission was a slight.

Then, again, there was the cost of their uniforms
and arms, which must be of the gayest on parade,
when they were playing at the soldiers' trade. The
wealthier among the members, we are told, were encouraged by the authorities to show their public feeling in promoting common interests, and so, doubtless,
spent their money freely to give *éclat* to their games
or their processions. The office of Gymnasiarch   Athletic
especially is recorded as the privilege of men of   sports.
means, who fostered the athletic sports; and if not

16 *University Life in Ancient Athens.*

in that respect, at least in others, may remind us of the captain of a modern cricket club, or of a College eight. *eleven? – football?*

Sconces. Something, too, there is which reads as if there had been sconces or fines imposed by the members on each other, in support of social rules or codes of honour; but these were looked on with disfavour from above, as likely to cause jars in the harmony of friendly intercourse; and one rector, at least, put them down.

The final examinations. At length the year drew to its close, and with it the restraints of discipline; but one ordeal still remained to try them. There is no new thing under the sun, and we find that there were examinations, even in old times, at Athens. Plutarch tells us by

Symp. Qu. ix. 1. the way that the Mayor on one occasion came to the gymnasium to examine the Ephebi 'who studied literature and geometry, rhetoric and music.' The ceremony ended with a public dinner to which all the college tutors were invited as well as lecturers and men of learning, but the guests, we read, were not so orderly in their behaviour as might have been expected. At the end of Term the town council was expected to attend, and hear the posers do their work; or, as we should say in modern language, the student

in the Senate-house. sat for examination in the Senate-house. There was, probably, no paper-work required, but only an oral apposition; it may be even that the phrase chiefly refers to some manual exercises or parade, more than to tests of intellectual progress. For we do not hear of any class-lists; or rather those we have, and they are full enough, contain the names only of the prizemen in the races and athletic sports, and do not deal with the cultivation of the mind.

Class-lists.

In any case they do not seem to have hurt themselves with their hard reading; the records insist upon the perfect health enjoyed by all the youths, as fully as if we had the extracts of a sanitary report. They were models, too, of good behaviour, those pattern students of old time, if we may trust the complimentary language of the marbles. They went to lectures steadily, and listened quietly to what was told them, and never rioted about the streets, or fell out in their cups like vulgar fellows in a drunken brawl, nor failed to do what their authorities enjoined, but ' were quite faultless all the long year through.'

Their healthy state

and good behaviour.

We may naturally ask who were the guardians of a discipline so perfect as to seem more fitly lodged in some cloister of Utopia.

The Head of the College held the title of *Cosmetes*, or of rector, and was assisted or replaced at times by a sub-rector; for so custom, though not law, required, since one at least declined to have a formal deputy, and preferred the assistance of his son.

The Cosmetes, or Head of the College.

C

There were also various instructors, too low in rank to be like tutors, though for convenience we may call them by that name. The Rector, appointed only for a year by popular election, was no merely honorary head, but took an important part in the real work of education. He was sometimes clothed with priestly functions; was, as we should say in Holy Orders; and never failed, so we are often told, to be present at religious service. He went to lectures even with the men, attending sometimes all the public courses with exemplary diligence. But that was not enough. He must go to drill with them at their volunteering; must visit, at their head, the watch-towers and outposts on the frontier, where the Ephebi had been posted in old days; he must look on at their gymnastic feats, and see that they were kept in proper training, and were very careful to avoid all coarse and indecorous language; and he must even take some part, as starter or as judge perhaps, in their boat-races.

He must be a man of substance, to play his part becomingly, for there were expenses which he could not well avoid. He often bore the cost himself of the religious services of his own College, paying for the victims for the sacrifice. He subscribed towards the silver plate which was the customary offering, and in other ways lightened the burdens on the students. When the outer wall of their gymnasium fell into ruins, the Rector of the day rebuilt it at his own expense; and though he thankfully accepted from his pupils the complimentary present of his statue, yet he did not forget to pay for it himself.

Some, however, of the work of supervision devolved upon the Sophronistæ, or the proctors, who were charged specially with the moral guidance of the youths, and to whose constant watchfulness the orderly behaviour often spoken of was largely due. The tutors, or instructors, were specialised, as we have seen, to definite work; each was told off to deal with a single set of muscles, or some physical aptitude or grace, and therefore they scarcely rose above the rank of trainers, or of fencing or dancing masters. At first appointed by each rector only for a year, they gradually obtained a longer hold upon their places, till they gained a sort of vested right, and held their offices for life.

The Sophronistæ, or proctors.

Tutors.

The Rector had his accounts at last to pass before official auditors appointed by the State. That done with credit, he might return to private life after one year of responsible routine; but he was seldom allowed to lay down office without some mark of honour, if he had done his duty faithfully, and not been too unpopular among his pupils. Some one in

The College accounts

the general assembly was sure to propose a vote of thanks, couched in the most complimentary terms, to the rector and all the officials of the year.

The vote of thanks in the public assembly.

The motion was carried without fail, and embodied formally in a decree. So flattering a proof of merit was not allowed to remain buried in the dusty archives. It was reproduced in more enduring form in stone, and posted, probably where all might read it, in the gymnasium of the College, whose walls were made to serve as a gazette of academic news.

The inscriptions or series of such votes.

The custom was observed from year to year, till the marble slabs spread over a large area of masonry; and as in course of time, by the ravages of war, or the processes of slow decay, the buildings crumbled into ruins, the storied fragments were strewn upon the ground and covered over, till history lost sight of them for ages. But gradually one after another reappeared; and, as the ardour of antiquarian research revived at Athens in our own days, a lengthy series was at length pieced together and arranged, extending, though not of course in an unbroken order, from the Macedonian period to the third century of our era. We may gain a clearer insight into the social manners of the times, if we take the trouble to read over one of the decrees as a characteristic member of the series in question. The document is dated from the 8th of the month Boedromion, and the year, as indi-

The College System.

cated by the Archon's name, belongs probably to the beginning of the first century before our era.

Aphrodisius, the son of Aphrodisius the Azenian, moved:—'That whereas the Ephebi of last year sacrificed duly at their matriculation in the Guildhall, by the sacred fire of the City, in the presence of their Rector and the Priests of the People and the Pontiffs, according to the laws and decrees, and conducted the procession in honour of Artemis the Huntress, ... and took part in others of like kind, and ran in the customary torch-races, and escorted the statue of Pallas to Phalerum, and helped to bring it back again, and light it on its way in perfect order, and carried Dionysus also from his shrine into the theatre in like fashion, and brought a bull worthy of the God at the Dionysiac festival, ... and took part in all due offerings to our Gods and our Benefactors, as the laws and the decrees ordain; and have been regular in their attendance all the year at the gymnasia, and punctually obeyed their Rector, thinking it of paramount importance to observe discipline, and to study diligently what the People has prescribed;—whereas there has been no ground for complaint, but they have kept all the rules made by their Rector and their Tutors, and have attended without fail the lectures of Zenodotus in the Ptolemæum and the Lyceum, as also those of all the

A vote of thanks as proposed in the Senate. Dumont Textes Eph. ii. 152.

other Professors of Philosophy in the Lyceum and Academy; and have mounted guard in good order at the popular assemblies, and have gone out to meet our Roman friends and benefactors on their visits; ... and have given 70 drachmæ, as the law provides, to the proper functionaries to provide the goblet for the Mother of the Gods, and offered another also in the temple at Eleusis; and have marched out under arms to the Athenian frontiers, and made themselves acquainted with the country and the roads, ... and have gone out to Marathon and offered their garlands and said prayers at the shrine of the heroes who died fighting for their country's freedom; ... and have gone on shipboard to the feast of Aiantæa, and held boat-races and processions there, and earned the praises of the Salaminians, and the present of a golden crown because of their good discipline and orderly behaviour;—and whereas they have lived in friendly harmony all the year without a jar as their Rector wished, and have passed their Examinations in the Senate House as the law requires; and being full of honourable ambition and desire to help their Rector in his public-spirited endeavours to promote the public good as well as their own credit, they have taken in hand one of the old catapults that was out of gear, and repairing it at their own expense, have learnt once more how to use the engine, the practice of which had been disused for years; and in all other matters have conducted themselves with all propriety, and have provided all that was required for the religious services of their own gymnasia—to show the wish of the Senate and the People to honour them for their merits and obedience to the laws and to their Rector, in their first year of adult life, the Senate is agreed to instruct the Presidents of the next assembly following, to lay before the People for approval the Resolution of the Senate to pass an honorary vote in praise of the Ephebi of last year, and to present them with a golden crown for their constant piety and discipline and public spirit, and to compliment their Tutors, their trainer Timon, and the fencing master Satyrus, and the marksman Nicander, and the bowman Asclepiades, and Calchedon the instructor in the catapults, and the attendants, and to award a crown of leaves to each; and to have the decree engraved by the Secretary for the time being on two pillars of stone, to be placed one in the Market-place, and the second wherever may seem best.'

Again, a few days afterwards, in a regular assembly in the theatre, one of the presidents put to the vote the following resolution of the Senate and the people:—' Whereas the People always has a hearty *A decree of the assembly.*

interest in the training and discipline of the Ephebi, hoping that the rising generation may grow up to be men able to take good care of their fatherland, and has passed laws to require them to gain a knowledge of the country, of the guardposts and of the frontiers, and to train themselves as soldiers in the use of arms, thanks to which discipline the City has been decked with many glories and imposing trophies; and whereas on this account the People has always chosen a Rector of unblemished character, and accordingly last year Dionysius the son of Socrates, the Phylasian, had the care of the Ephebi entrusted to him by the People, and duly sacrificed with them at their matriculation, . . . and has trained them worthily, keeping them constantly engaged at the gymnasia, and making them all efficient in their drill, and insisting on decorum, that they should not fail throughout the year in obedience to the Generals, the Tutors and himself; and whereas he has watched over their habits of order and of self-control, taking them with him to the Professors' Lectures, and being present always at their courses of instruction . . . and whereas he has also roused their public spirit by teaching them to be good marksmen with the catapult, and accompanied them in their rounds to the guardposts and the frontiers . . . and has arranged the boat-races in the processions at Munychia . . . and also the footraces in the gymnasia, and the escorts of honour for our Roman friends and allies . . . and reviewed them on parade at the Theseia and Epitaphia . . . and has been vigilant in all cases to maintain their pride, being constant in attendance on them through the year, and has watched over their studies, and ruled them with impartial justice, keeping them in sound health and friendly intercourse, treating them with a father's care—in return for all of which the Ephebi have presented him with a golden crown and a bronze statue, to show their sense of his character and loving care; and whereas he has passed his accounts as the law requires, the Senate and the People wishing to show due honour to such Rectors as serve with merit and impartiality, Resolve to praise Dionysius, late Rector of the Ephebi of last year and to present him with a golden crown, and have proclamation made thereof in the great festival of Dionysus, as also at the athletic contests of the Panathanaic and Eleusinian feasts.'

In conclusion we may briefly note

1. The system of education thus described was under the control of the government throughout. *The system above described was a national one under the control of the State.*

'The laws and the decrees' were constantly appealed to in the records, not as guaranteeing corporate status, or securing rights of property, but as organising and defining all the essentials of the institution. They insisted that a religious influence should be exerted, prescribing even the ritual established by the State; they claimed the right to interfere with the details, to correct and to reward the chief officials. It was a truly national system under government inspection, though largely supplemented by voluntary action.

Our information is drawn almost exclusively from the inscriptions,

2. It may surprise us that our information comes almost entirely from the inscriptions, and that ancient writers are all nearly silent on the subject. The later Athenian comedy, indeed, if that were left to us, would probably refer to it in illustration of the social manners of the times. But there was little to attract the literary circles in arrangements so mechanical and formal; there was too much of outward pageantry, and too little of real character evolved; the professorial teaching was a mere excrescence of the system; the Rectors passed so rapidly across the stage that none could stamp any marked impress of his genius on it; and originality must have been cramped by the strait-waistcoat of rigid forms.

which are minute in their details,

3. Strangely enough, our information does not end even with all the complimentary phrases, of which a sample has been given in the foregoing decree. There is specified sometimes the exact number of the members of the College; and more

The College System.

or less lengthy fragments are still left of the muster rolls, in which the proper names and the nationalities of each are stated. The native-born and aliens are distinguished in the different lists; the varying proportions serve to mark the times when this special type of education rose and fell in popular esteem elsewhere. In the second century of our era when more than one hundred strangers sometimes matriculated in the same year, only two or three Roman names occur, while the great towns of Asia Minor and the isles of the Ægean are constantly appearing. The Roman character was still too unimaginative and commonplace to prize the varied attractiveness of life at Athens. But the Syrian populations flocked to her, the men of Ascalon and Berytus above all, disguising partially their native names in a Greek dress. It is of special interest to note that at the very time when a new religious influence was spreading from the East, there is so much evidence of fusion between the Greek and the Semitic culture. In the last the Jews played probably no unimportant part; they abounded in all the marts of trade and crowded cities; and, as in the Middle Ages at the schools of Cordova and Bagdad, they may have served to some extent as dragomans between the East and West. But only a small proportion of such foreign students

giving the numbers and names of the students,

and showing that there were many of Semitic race.

entered as Ephebi, for the out-College system seemingly was most in favour, and of the multitudes who flocked to Athens, and stayed there for long years, by far the most were unattached, choosing their own course of reading and their private tutors, without any check of examinations or degrees. It is time to turn to the character and methods of their studies, and to deal with the larger and the most important sections of our subject.

CHAPTER II.

THE PROFESSORS OF PHILOSOPHY.

FEW subjects in Athenian history are better known than the characteristic features of the four great schools of thought, which differently developed the same Socratic teaching. This is not the place to describe their principles or method, or to ask how it was that such divergent streams of influence as those which flowed from Plato and from Aristotle, from Epicurus and from Zenon, can be ultimately traced to the same fountain head. But it is more important for us to enquire how each maintained its separate existence, and organised itself in outward forms through which it acted on the world.

The four great schools of thought.

One of the first needs was, in each case, a sort of authorised version of their philosophic creed; but the written word was not enough: the writings of their founder, canonical as they might be, could not content them; they must have a living voice to expand and illustrate the truth, to stimulate by the contagious influence of strong conviction, and meet

The system of succession in the masters of each school, objections from all quarters. It is not too much to say, perhaps, that they believed in a sort of Apostolical succession in their midst. Each master of the school was the living guardian of the Ark of Truth, in the fulness of an undivided trust, to be supreme in matters of the Faith.

Each handed on the lighted torch to his successor, that the sacred fire of truth might not be spent; each, probably, believed himself to be the depository of unchanged traditions, though all the world of thought was on the move. He chose commonly another who might fill his place when he was gone. Sometimes he waited till his death-bed, sometimes before the ruling spirit passed away, the prophet's mantle fell on his successor's shoulders. Sometimes in his will he named a follower to replace him; or even put the office in commission for awhile, till the trusty few had made their choice. Once made, it *religiously respected by the chief members of the sect.* seems to have been religiously respected by the rest. Some jealous criticism there may, perhaps, have been at times, by spirits more than commonly impatient; but it was seldom that any ventured to dispute his claims to their obedience, or to set up a rival oracle beside him. Many even of the greatest names appear to have waited quietly as greybeards, till a vacancy was made by death, and they were called to assume the foremost place.

Of the long list of names recorded in the biographies of Diogenes Laertius, we hear only of one who set up for himself, when the head of his school was still alive. Chrysippus had so much vanity of self-assertion, or was so full of missionary zeal, that he made himself a master of the conferences while Cleanthes was still living. But in later days, we are told, he rued his fault, and owned that the one thing which he regretted was undutiful behaviour to his teacher. Another, Crantor, withdrew himself on grounds of health from the friendly company of sages, and it was expected that he would ere long be heard of as an independent teacher at the Asclepeium; but, the cure effected, he returned to the old lecture-halls, to swell the audience of his chief, till he was called at last to take the lead. D. L. vii. 7. 1. D. L. iv. 5. 4.

We have seen already that they chose for their lectures and discussions the public buildings which were called gymnasia, of which there were several in different quarters of the city. They could only use them by the sufferance of the State, which had built them chiefly for bodily exercises and athletic feats. We do not hear if the trainers and the fencing masters resented the intrusion of the throngs of students, though it is likely that there were chances of collision. But we do hear, in one case, of complaints that their neighbours were disturbed. One They lectured in the public gymnasia.

Gymnasiarch, or curator of the hall, had to beg Carneades not to talk so loudly to his pupils, as he was annoying other folks. 'How loudly may I speak, then?' said the lecturer, in impatience. 'Loud enough for your audience to hear,' was the retort; and perhaps the audience was not large, and the retort was somewhat sharp. Before long several of the schools drew themselves apart in special buildings, and even took their most familiar names, such as the Lyceum and the Academy, from the gymnasia, in which they made themselves at home.

Gradually we find the traces of some material provisions, which helped to define and to perpetuate the different sects. Plato had a little garden, close by the sacred Eleusinian Way, in the shady groves of the Academy, which he bought, says Plutarch, for some 3,000 drachmæ.

There lived also his successors, Xenocrates and Polemon, the former of whom spent there so much the life of a recluse, as to leave it only for a single day each year, at the festival of the greater Dionysia, when the new plays were acted; while the latter gathered pupils round him, who listened to him as he walked under the trees, and who even had their little huts built there to live as near as might be round his garden. It was but a tiny glebe at first; but wealthier friends of learning added from time to time to the domain, or bequeathed in their wills the funds which provided for the chief philosophers of Plato's school a quiet life of independent means.

Aristotle, as we know, in later life had taught in the Lyceum, in the rich grounds near the Ilissus, and there he probably possessed the house and garden which after his death came into the hands of his successor, Theophrastus. The latter in his will disposed of them as follows:—'My garden and the walk, and all the buildings which adjoin the glebe, I bequeath to such of my friends, herein described, who care to pass their lives in them together in study and philosophy, on condition that no one shall alienate or make any individual claim; but that all shall share alike, and live in domestic peace together, as is natural and right.' Then follow the names of ten of his most trusted friends, and among them that of Straton, who replaced him. Straton, in his turn, left the studio to Lycon, 'for the rest are too old or too busy; yet they will but do their duty if they strengthen his hands with kindly help.' Lycon bequeathed the garden walk to ten of his friends in trust, and bade them raise to the first place whoever seemed most likely to persevere and to promote the interests of the sect. He also asked the rest of the connexion to lend their aid out of regard to him as well as to the local ties.

Suidas, s. v. Πλάτων.

In the Aristotelian.

D. L. v. 2. 14.

D. L. v. 3. 7.

<small>In the Epicurean.</small>

The famous garden of Epicurus in the outer Keramicus, which he bought for eighty minæ, was a quiet resting-place, not for himself only, but for the friends who gathered there for shelter in hard times, to see how simply the advocate of pleasure lived. He left it at his death for the members of his school, as the will tells us, which Diogenes Laertius records:—

<small>D. L. x. 10. 10.</small>

'I give my property in trust to Amynomachus and Timocrates on the condition that they make over the use of the garden, and all that it contains, to Hermarchus, and those who join his speculations, and to such as he may choose to take his place, that they may there give themselves to study; and, moreover, I beg all who take their principles from me to do their best as a solemn trust to help Amynomachus and Timocrates to maintain the school buildings in my garden, and their heirs after them, as also those who may be appointed to replace my own successors. And let my executors allow Hermarchus and his fellow students to inhabit my house in Melite as long as he shall live. And out of the funds bequeathed by me I will that my executors, in concert with Hermarchus, provide religious services for my father and mother and brothers and myself, . . . and also for the stated meeting to be held on the 20th of every month by all the members of my sect.' The possessions here disposed of seem to have remained for centuries the property of all the sect of Epicurus, and though the Garden, and the groves of the Academy, were wasted sometimes by the ravages of war, exposed as they were without the walls, yet in the later days of Cicero those haunts of old philosophy were often visited by pious pilgrims. The sentence last quoted from the will of Epicurus may remind us that, besides the common property in house and lands, some funds were also set apart to keep the student world together.

It seems a natural thing in our own days to think that men must dine together when they would promote some common interest in politics or art or science, and every company or club must have at least its annual dinner. The custom is a very old one, and even philosophy took kindly to the practice. Athenæus, after speaking of all the civic banquets held by every tribe and ward and borough, goes on to note that 'there are many meetings of philosophers in the city, some called the pupils of Diogenes, and others pupils of Antipater, others, again, styled disciples of Panætius. And Theophrastus bequeathed money for an entertainment of that sort. Not, of course, that the sages so assembled might give way to intemperance, but in order that they might enjoy a wise and learned conversation at the feast. . . . The philosophers used to take pains to collect the

Endowments for philosophic dinners;

Deipn. v. 2.

young men, and as they supped with them to observe some law which was carefully defined. Accordingly there were rules for banquets laid down by Xenocrates, in the Academy, and by Aristotle also.' But either the rules were very lax, or they were broken before long, if we may trust what Athenæus tells us in another place. 'When Lycon became the chief man in the Peripatetic school, he used to entertain his friends at dinner with unusual extravagance and pride. . . . He had a room large enough to hold twenty couches, in the most fashionable quarter of the city. Besides the music provided for his feasts, and the silver plate and coverlets which were displayed, the dishes were so sumptuous, and the tables and the cooks so many, that people were alarmed, and shrunk away in fear, although they wished to be admitted to his school. . . . For the members were required to take in turn the office of chief manager, and the duties of this office were to superintend the novices for thirty days, . . . and then on the last day of the month, to receive from each nine obols, and to entertain at supper not only those who paid their quota, but all those whom Lycon might invite, as well as those among the elders who were punctual in attending lectures; so that the money which was paid them did not go far enough to pay even for the unguents and the flowers.

[margin: which tended to become extravagant. xii. 69.]

... Plato and Speusippus had not instituted these that folks might sit till daybreak at the festive board ... but that men might seem to honour Heaven, and live naturally with one another, and chiefly that they might enjoy a natural rest and conversation, all which became quite secondary in their eyes to soft clothes, and extravagant self-indulgence.' It was perhaps one symptom of decline in moral earnestness when the philosophers accepted the large donations of Antigonus Gonatas, for a great dinner on the anniversary of his son's death. They waved their differences of creed, we hear, and dined together in good fellowship, and each master of the schools became in turn the chairman at the banquet; but now and then their jealous antipathies could not be soothed, and one at least, we read of, Lycon, would not accept the invitation to a rival's table. [D. L. iv. 6. 17.] [D. L. v. 4. 4.]

As yet we have seen no forms of State endowment, nor even any legal recognition of the corporate status of the sects. Sometimes the little property was possessed by their head in his own right, though with a tacit understanding that he should leave it to his next successor, sometimes it was held in trust for the benefit of the connexion, like modern chapels on the congregational system. The principal members, too, were something like the deacons, and could at times appoint, if not dismiss their spiritual head. [No legal recognition of corporate rights in the sects.]

They resented any interference from the State.
D. L. v. 2. 5.

So jealous were they of their independence as to resent the least show of interference from the State, somewhat as priests resent at times in matters of the faith any appeal to secular tribunals. On one occasion, as we read, a crisis in politics was followed by a liberal reaction, which found little favour with the thinkers nursed in theories like those of Plato; a law was passed in haste, at the motion of one Sophocles, which made it penal for any one to open school, or give any sort of public lectures, without the sanction of the State. The students soon were in high dudgeon when they heard that the liberty of instruction was thus narrowed, and they resolved to migrate in a body from a city so intolerant of intellectual freedom. Theophrastus, then in the zenith of his fame, and counting his pupils by the thousand, sympathised with the movement, and seceded with his scholars, till Athens realising speedily how much her attraction and renown depended on her academic throngs, repealed the unlucky law in haste, and sued them humbly to return.

Some of the philosophers were men of substance, and could easily maintain themselves in studious ease, while others found their little means eked out by the help of the small endowments lately mentioned. But besides this nearly all accepted presents at the hands of those who came to hear them.

Socrates, indeed, had spoken strongly against what seemed to him a sordid and a mercenary practice, for wisdom was too infinitely precious to be appraised at any money value. His own immediate followers and friends shared probably his sentiment, and taught in the true missionary spirit. But before long the prejudice grew weaker; and Speusippus, Plato's immediate successor, was taunted with disloyalty to his own master's principles, in ' exacting tribute from all whether they would or no.' Xenocrates, indeed, adhered more faithfully to old traditions, and declined nearly all the presents sent to him, even by crowned heads, though he was so poor that he was sold on one occasion when he cou'd not pay the taxes, and owed his freedom to the liberal friend of learning, Demetrius Phalereus. But it soon became a recognised thing that, even in the field of science the labourer was worthy of his hire, though so late as the days of Lucian it was thought unworthy of a grave professor to make much ado about his fees, or appeal to the law courts to enforce the payment.

The fees paid by students.

D. L. iv. 1. 5.

D. L. iv. 2. 5.

D. L. iv. 2. 10.

Lucian, Hermotimus.

Yet there was one sect, the Cynic or the Stoic, which for many generations discouraged all endowments, and would accept little or nothing from the living. At first its members aimed at nothing more than the means of bare subsistence, and like Crates when smitten with the love of wisdom, sold what

The Cynic or Stoic sect discouraged endowments and fees.

they had in the spirit of the sainted Francis, and gave the money all away, as only a hindrance in the perfect way of life. The scholars who gathered round them were often of the poorest, like Cleanthes, who turned the miller's wheel by night to earn a scanty pittance, that he might have leisure to attend the public courses in the day. They often did their best to drive away from them the wealthy or fastidious, by putting them to irksome tasks, like Zenon, who was bidden to carry a pot of porridge through the streets, and when he felt ashamed and hid it in his cloak, had a blow from his master's stick which broke the pot and spilt the mess over his clothes.

D. L. vi. 5. 4.

D. L. vii. 5. 2.

D. L. vii. 1. 3.

The large number of students of philosophy.

Yet in spite of all discouragements the students of philosophy increased, and rich and poor crowded alike to the lecture halls of the Professors. Theophrastus, for example, had as many as 2,000 pupils. For the passion of speculative thought was fresh and vigorous in Greece, though the currents of free life were flowing feebly; as the confidence was shaken in the old standards of authority and State enactments, men turned with eagerness to systems which promised to make them a law unto themselves; the earnest-minded crowded round the sages as in the Middle Ages men were drawn to the cloister or to the lectures of the Schoolmen, to get more light on the eternal problems of man's destiny, or to find an intellectual excitement in a subtle dialectic.

We may take as typical the story which we read of Zenon, visiting Athens for purposes of trade, and lighting at a bookseller's shop on the Socratic Memoirs, which he pored over with increasing interest till he asked at length 'Where are such men to be found?' and at once attached himself to Crates, who was pointed out to him close by. The call to Philosophy in his case, as in that of many another, reads like the stories of conversion to religion, or like the sudden resolution to renounce the world as Monk or Nun. *[Stories of sudden conversion. D. L. vii. 1. 3.]*

Athens, though she maintained no Chairs as yet, was proud of the distinguished teachers who made a home within her walls. She felt a pride in her Hellenic name, which was becoming through the world synonymous with mental cultivation. She welcomed gracefully the strangers who came to sit at the feet of famous sages; she insisted on the attendance at their lectures of the Ephebi whose studies she controlled by law; and when a great man died among them, alien though he was like Zenon, she honoured him with a solemn vote of thanks, and decreed him a public funeral as a 'good man who had done his best to form the character of his young hearers, and lead them on to manliness and self-restraint by showing his own practice to be always in harmony with his professions.' *[Honorary recognition of the philosophers by Athens. Isocrates Paneg. 50. D. L. vii. 1. 9.]*

Little endowment as yet needed.

So for ages little or no endowment of research was needed, while the passion for knowledge was intense; and multitudes who had little taste for earnest thought still flocked as a thing of course to Athens to get a sort of educational finish, or to gain a familiarity at second-hand with the great speculative questions of the day. To some study was its own reward, and they could live contentedly on little. Others who set up for Professors, and were ready to instruct all comers, could reap rich harvests, if they cared, from the payments of their willing pupils.

Rival seats of learning for other branches of study.

But it was only in philosophy that the schools of Athens reigned supreme. Other intellectual rivals were growing into note meantime, and were able to assert their separate claims.

Alexandria had her royal founder, to build and endow a great museum with cloisters, dining-hall, and library, and salaried professors who were perhaps not always bound to lecture, but might give themselves to study unhampered by restrictions, and swell the gathered store of knowledge, and stimulate mainly by example. Here were able critics, great in canons of prosody and rules of taste; poets whose facile muse was at times somewhat overweighted by its learning; geometers who carried to the furthest the Greek subtlety of deductive thought; geographers who arrayed in scientific form the tales of travellers and explorers. Rhodes, although no more the mistress of the sea, had her famous schools of rhetoric, in which Cicero stayed awhile for study. Scarcely less skilful in the play of dialectic were the teachers who abounded in the great towns of Asia Minor. Tarsus is singled out by Strabo as a seat of learning, whose citizens had the most unselfish love of letters. Marseilles, again, was fast becoming the favourite resort of studious Romans.

Strabo, iv. 10. 13.

Here were formidable rivals to compete with the doctors of the Porch and the Academy. For a time, probably, the influence of Athens rested mainly on the associations of the past, or the artistic beauties of a city peopled with so many memories dear to thoughtful minds. It is thus that Cicero, in his later years, speaks of the recollections of his visits to those scenes: 'After hearing Antiochus in the Ptolemæum, in the company of Piso and my brother and Pomponius and my cousin Lucius, for whom I had a brother's love, we agreed to take our evening walk in the Academy, chiefly because that spot would be the least crowded at that time. So we all met at Piso's house, as was agreed, and, chatting as we went, walked the six stadia, between the Gate Dipylum and the Academy. When we reached the scenes so justly famous, we found the quietude we craved.

The influence of old associations in favour of Athens.

De Finibus, v. 1.

"Is it a natural sentiment," asked Piso, " or a mere illusion, which makes us more affected when we see the spots frequented by men worth remembering, than when we merely hear their deeds or read their works? It is thus that I feel touched at present, for I think of Plato, who, as we are told, was wont to lecture here. Not only do those gardens of his, close by, remind me of him, but I seem to fancy him before my eyes. Here stood Speusippus, here Xenocrates, here his hearer Polemon...." "Yes," said Quintus, " what you say, Piso, is quite true, for as I was coming hither, Colonus, yonder, called my thoughts away, and made me fancy that I saw its inmate Sophocles, for whom you know my passionate admiration...." "And I too," said Pomponius, " whom you often attack for my devotion to Epicurus, spend much time in his garden, which we passed lately in our walk."'

Yet her attractive power grew weaker.

But, in spite of old associations, the attractiveness of Athens had declined, and the student world no longer crowded to her as before. The ravages of war had swept over the land, the siege of Sulla had laid waste the groves of Plato, and the garden in which Epicurus lived; the civil strife left little time for peaceful studies, and the early empire showed no favour to the home of letters, where Brutus and even Antony had loved to court a brief respite from the din of war. The sages, indeed, had soon returned with quiet times to the old haunts, and Cicero was surprised to see how little they cared for the havoc that was made; but philosophy had spent, for a time at least, its force of active speculation, and was living on its hoarded capital; as such it had less charm for earnest minds; other centres, other studies beguiled away the growing manhood of the age, and, as Strabo says, the young noblemen of Rome forgot the way to Athens and betook themselves to Gaul. iv. 1. 5.

But the old city raised its head again, thanks to the magnificent patronage of Hadrian, who honoured it with marked affection, and deserved by his liberality some at least of the pompous phrases in which the Greeks spoke of him in inscriptions, as 'founder, benefactor, restorer of the world.' The Antonines did even more for it in the interests of learning. With them began the system of endowments by the State; some of the lecturers became recognised Professors, and the University existed as by law established. Few precise details are given us in ancient authors of the number and the value of the imperial appointments. Dion Cassius tells us, in vague language, that the philosophic Emperor Marcus 'gave salaried teachers to the world at Athens in every branch of letters.' From Lucian it

Margin notes: It revived, thanks to the patronage of Hadrian, and the Antonines, who began the system of state endowments. 71, 81.

would seem that a round sum of 10,000 drachmæ was allotted to at least one representative in each of the four great schools, to say nothing of lecturers in other subjects, who will be mentioned presently. Stoic as the Emperor was himself, he was so tolerant as to wish all other systems to have fair play and equal favour. He was competent enough to choose the ablest men, but he allowed the brilliant Herodes Atticus to have the disposal of his patronage. After his death, if we may trust Lucian's lively pictures, a board of electors filled the vacant places, and the Satirist describes them as grave and reverend seniors, before whom the competitors appeared in person to make good their title to the vacant chair ($\theta\rho\acute{o}\nu os$), and to prove their fitness by actual display, like candidates in these days preaching their trial sermons for a vacant living. The field was gradually narrowed, till only two were left, like athletes, to dispute the victory. Each made parade of all his erudition, his mastery of the logic of his school, to prove himself the fittest representative of Aristotle's doctrines. But they warmed to their work, as they went on, and leaving the passionless theories of dialectic, they betook themselves to virulent invective, not shrinking from personalities the most grotesque, and the most unsavoury charges. The scene described is too absurd to be literally true, though it may point to some unseemly

Lucian's description of an election by a board. Eunuchus.

passages in the appointments of the board. Yet we may fairly balance this unfavourable picture by another which the same writer paints for us, in far more flattering colours. He puts into the mouth of one Nigrinus an elaborate eulogy of Athens: 'Brought up as are the citizens in philosophy and poverty, they never look with favour on a neighbour or a stranger who tries to bring in luxury among them. Far from that, if anyone arrives among them with such habits, they try to convert him by degrees, and school him imperceptibly till they bring him to a better mind. He told me how a wealthy upstart came in vulgar pomp to Athens, expecting to be envied and admired for his crowds of servants and his clothes of broidered gold; but they only pitied the poor wretch, and tried to correct him in a kindly way, not blaming him rudely to his face, as in their free city anyone may live as he thinks best. But when he annoyed them at the gymnasia or the baths, by crowding them with all his slaves, one of them whispered to his neighbour, as if he did not wish the man to hear, "He is afraid of being murdered at his bath, yet all is perfectly secure, and there is no need of an armed force." The stranger heard the plain truth, and took the hint. And so they made him put aside his embroidery and purple by their sly remarks upon the flowery colours. "Why, here we

A more favourable picture in same author of Athenian society.

Lucian. Nigrinus.

have the spring already," said one; "where does this peacock come from?" said another. "Surely, he has put on his mother's gown,' a third; and so on with like pleasantries. In this way too they made their jokes about his many rings and perfumed locks and extravagance of manner, till they brought him to a sounder state, and sent him home the better for his schooling. . . . Nigrinus praised, besides, the freedom which prevailed in Athens, the absence of all jealousy, the tranquil leisure which they enjoy so fully. He showed me how a course so ordered is in agreement with philosophy, and can preserve its moral purity; and that nothing can be better suited to a man of virtue, who does not care for riches, but is resolved to live a natural and honest life.'

It is true that the picture may be overcoloured from the wish to bring out more into relief, by way of contrast, the affectation and the vice of Rome. But we may turn to a less questionable witness, and read the pleasant memoirs of his student life at Athens, with which Aulus Gellius relieves the dulness of his pedantry. In them we shall find portrayed a simplicity of habits, and an unaffected interest in moral progress which were rare seemingly elsewhere. He tells us most of Taurus the philosopher, who was not content with formal lectures, but did his best to form the character of his young

as also in Aulus Gellius.

friends by personal converse, chatting with them at his bedroom door when they had walked home with him from lecture, travelling with them sometimes in the country, taking long walks to see them when he heard that they were sick, and whiling away their weariness by pleasant talk, in which the serious mingled with the gay. If he asked his pupils to his table he did not care to tempt the appetite with costly viands, but the simple fare of pudding or of salad was seasoned with true Attic salt, and his guests were happier and wiser when they left him. He had a way of delicately hinting that a fault might be mended or bad habit dropped, which served its end, while it spared his hearer's self-respect. Yet Taurus was no easy going teacher, with a standard easily attained. He liked to tell his youthful friends the story of Euclides, who braved death to hear Socrates, his friend and guide, when it was penal for one of Megara to enter Athens; whereas nowadays, he said, philosophers must often wait till their pupils have recovered from the wine party of the night before. He reproached them also for their want of earnestness and depth; told them that they wanted to pick and choose, to gather here a thought and there a hint, somewhat as lecturers in our days at times complain that undergraduates are too practically minded, and read not for the sake of knowledge,

Aulus Gellius, ii. 2.

xii. 5.

xviii. 10.

xvii. 8.

xx. 4.

vi. 10.

i. 9.

E

but a class. The same writer also dwells upon the pleasant memories of Kephissia, where among leafy groves and murmuring cascades Herodes Atticus kept open house, and entertained the students with dignified and courteous refinement. Munificent patron of the arts and letters, and acknowledged leader of the Academic world, he was at home alike in the flowery paths of rhetoric and the gravest themes of speculation, and was at once Philosopher and Sophist. He had his passages of Epictetus ready to silence the conceited braggart who set up for a Stoic oracle on the strength of a little captious dialectic, and a few learned phrases caught up at second hand. He had no mercy on the Cynic who rudely pushed in, demanding alms of right, and grumbling because he was not recognised as a compeer. 'A beard and staff indeed I see,' was the retort, 'but no philosopher.'

But he was too much of the 'grand seigneur' to be accepted as the type of the Greek sage, contented with a modest lot. Much indeed of his colossal fortune was expended on stately works to beautify the towns of Greece. But there does seem too much of personal display in his royal road to spelling, planned for the sake of his own backward child. He had, so runs the story, a number of his humble friends, each representing a different letter of the alphabet, to move about and form themselves into varying groups, to show the little dullard how to spell, somewhat as our journals tell us that a Viceroy of India may play at chess. He was a little too intent to reign supreme over the schools of Athens among the Professors of his own electing, as a sort of Chancellor by Imperial favour. Woe to the unlucky rhetorician who had not paid his court with due respect, or who presumed to air his brilliant periods without permission. A hint was quite enough to the young students in the theatre, and they clamoured the poor lecturer down, just as impatient lads at times drown the voice of the Public Orator at Oxford. At last men learnt to take his measure, and to get over him with guile. The famous Aristides, who was asked to pronounce the Panathenaic speech, read him the preamble in a draft which was so spiritless and tame as to disarm all jealous fears, but when the day came for the state display the real speech proved to be the author's masterpiece.

But indeed it must be owned that with all the endowment of research we hear too little of quiet study or of keenness of original speculation. The great names and moving powers are found elsewhere. Epictetus and Marcus Aurelius at Rome; Plutarch at Chæroneia, and Dion the Golden Mouthed in many a distant city, these probed deepest into the mysteries of life, or guided best the wavering

But there are few signs of originality or deep study at Athens.

conscience. Philosophy meantime had left the cloisters and the garden, and gone out in Stoic guise among the busy haunts of men. Sometimes she spoke with true missionary fervour, pleading with rude energy to every class without distinction, but talking mainly in the people's tongue. Sometimes, if we trust the Satirist Lucian, she condescended to questionable shifts, in the person of the spiritual confessors in great houses, submitting to the impertinence of vulgar upstarts, or attending the titled lady at her toilette, and whispering ghostly admonitions in her ear, as the maid brought in the billet-doux, or lavishing their care on the poodle of their mistress, when the little poodles were expected to appear.

<small>Lucian περὶ τῶν ἐπὶ μισθῷ.</small>

Sometimes her tenets might be heard from the mouth of Cynic vagrants, who moved about the world with staff and wallet, like the begging friars of a later age, but dragging often high professions through the mud. The four great sects were represented still at Athens, as we have seen, with their salaried Professors in their Chairs; but the ancient doctrines were rather themes for rhetorical expansion, than problems for serious thought, or rules of manly life. Henceforth the name of Sophist is the literary term for nearly all the public teachers, and there is little seeming difference of method or of aims between Philosophers and Rhetoricians, with the latter of whom we now proceed to deal.

CHAPTER III.

THE PROFESSORS OF RHETORIC.

IN the pages of Philostratus and of Eunapius, we see the Sophists pass in a long line before us, the same at Athens as at Antioch, or Smyrna, or many another seat of learning and of fashion, and for several centuries their characteristic features scarcely change.

The Sophists or profes-ors of rhetoric.

It was the old name that was revived, but with none of that undercurrent of contempt which the writings of the Socratic school had introduced into Greek thought. The older Sophists had their systems to explain the problems of the world around them; they mostly had their principles of metaphysics, however shallow they might seem to deeper reasoners like Plato. The new were mainly literary artists, playing on the chords of human feeling, laying under contribution poetry, and art, and ethics in their impartial interest in telling images and useful tropes.

Never was rhetoric so much in vogue; never were such enthusiastic crowds assembled round men to whom the manner was of vital moment, while they cared infinitely little for the matter of the thought. There were hundreds ready to compete for the Chairs *The public professors,* at Athens, whenever they were vacant, and if it were of interest, we might make out the list of those who filled them in succession. Two of this kind were specially endowed: one from imperial funds, the other by the city, and worth respectively ten thousand drachmæ and a talent. But besides these, as in other seats of fashion, there were many private teachers, *the private lecturers,* who gathered an audience round them as they could, and at times even eclipsed the salaried Professors.

At Athens, so few out of the Academic world *generally aliens.* were native born, that there seemed good reason for *Philostratus, ii. 62.* the fears of purists like Herodes, who complained that such a multitude of strangers had corrupted the purity of the Attic tongue, and only here and there, from a hermit in the country, could the old dialect be heard in all its beauty.

With many it was far from being a question of *Often men of wealth and rank.* a mere livelihood to gain. To say nothing of the princely manners of Herodes, the wealthiest of living men, many were of noble birth, and filled high office in their several states, or were entrusted with weighty diplomatic duties.

Aliens even rose to posts of honour, like Lollianus, the first occupant of the Athenian Chair, who was made *Strategus* or Mayor by the admiring city, and had the charge not of the arsenals as in old days of freedom, but of the markets and the corn trade. It would seem, however, that he was less at home in these new duties than in his lecture hall, for once we read, when there was a riot round the baker's shop, the populace began to pelt him, and were going on to worse, when a bystander brought them to their senses by exclaiming, 'Nay, Lollianus only deals in words, not loaves.'

Phil. ii. 39.

To some it seemed the highest object of ambition to rise to distinction as a Sophist, and feel that a great audience was hanging on their words. They could not stay long in their native homes, if they felt that they were capable of greater things, but must go forth into the larger world to air their talents and measure themselves with rivals of renown. Clazomenæ had hoped, indeed, that Scopelianus would remain at home, and lend a lustre to their little town, but he said in somewhat mocking jest, 'The caged bird will not sing,' and betook himself to fashionable Smyrna, whither the youth of all the neighbouring countries flocked to hear him.

Phil. ii. 2 .

Often they wandered off from land to land, to engage in literary tournaments with the champions whom they met, offering to lecture on some startling thesis, or to improvise on any that was given.

ii. 118.
The story of Hippodromus to illustrate the knight-errantry of the Sophists.

The following story in Philostratus may serve to illustrate the habit. Hippodromus, afterwards appointed to a professorship at Athens, came for the first time to Smyrna, and as soon as he had landed, walked straight to the market-place, to get a local guide. He saw a temple on his way, by which some private tutors sat, with servants carrying bundles of books under their arms, and guessed that there was somebody of note lecturing within. He walked inside and found Megistias, whom he bowed to without saying more. Megistias, thinking that it was a father or a guardian come to talk to him about a pupil, asked him what his errand was, but he only said, 'I will tell you when we are by ourselves.' When he had catechised the lads, the teacher said, 'now tell me what you want.' 'Let us exchange clothes,' was the answer of Hippodromus, who had on a travelling suit, while the other wore a lecturer's gown. 'Why do you ask that?' 'Because I wish to give you a specimen of my skill.' Megistias thought the stranger must be mad for talking in that style, but seeing that his face was quite composed he handed him his gown, and gave him a thesis as he asked. The other sat down on the chair, and thought a moment, then started up so suddenly as to make Megistias feel sure again that he was mad. But soon after he began his speech, the listener, full

The Professors of Rhetoric.   57

of admiration, hurried up, and begged to know who he could be. 'I am Hippodromus, the Thessalian,' he answered, 'and I have come here for experience, to see by the example of one man of learning in what style men lecture in Ionia, but let me finish my own speech.' Hardly had he done so, when all the educated men in Smyrna came hurrying to where Megistias was, for the rumour had already spread, that Hippodromus had come to visit them. So he took up the same subject, and handled it again in a new style, and afterwards came out in public, and filled them all with admiration.

So too we read of Marcus of Byzantium coming unawares into the room where Polemon was busy with his pupils. The stranger had a rustic look, for his beard and head were all unkempt and shaggy. But some one of the students who had visited Byzantium, remembering his face, whispered his name to his next neighbour, and so on till they knew all round. So when the lecturer called as usual for a theme, they all looked to where Marcus sat, expecting him to name one. 'Why are you staring at the bumpkin,' said their tutor, 'how can he start a subject?' Whereupon Marcus raised his voice and said, 'I will name a theme, and improvise upon it also.' His broad Doric at once betrayed him to his hearer, and they soon began to show off before each other, and parted at last with mutual admiration.

Phil. ii. 41. The story of Marcus of Byzantium.

The people commonly was nothing loath to hear; they streamed as to a popular preacher in our own day, or an actor starring in provincial towns: the epicures accepted the invitation to the feast of words, and hurried to the theatre to judge as critics the choice of images, and refinement of the style, and all the harmony of balanced periods.

<small>Popular enthusiasm for the Sophists.</small>

Few could resist the intoxication of applause. Aristides even, when the Emperor asked to hear him lecture, made it a condition that his friends might come to listen, and clap and shout as loud as they should please. Of course their heads were often turned with such applause: of course they gave themselves high airs, and many a story illustrates the boastful arrogance of the great sophists. Polemon began a speech at Athens with the words, 'You have the credit, Athenians, for being skilful judges of good style. I shall now see if you deserve it.' He carried indeed so far his self-assertion as to turn a future Emperor out of doors, when he came home unexpectedly, and found him quartered in his house by order of the council. Adrian, of Tyre, was not much humbler, for he began his inaugural address, on his appointment to a Chair at Athens, with the prelude, 'Once more come letters from Phœnicia.' Like some others of the class, he also showed his pride and ostentation in his outer man. He wore

<small>Phil. ii. 88.</small>

<small>Their vanity</small>

<small>Phil. ii. 46.</small>

<small>Phil. ii. 91.</small>

<small>and ostentation.</small>

the costliest clothes and rarest stones, and rode on state occasions in a carriage, the horses of which had silver bits. The ceremony over, he was escorted home by students from all parts of Greece, who treated him with all the reverence due to a High Priest at the Mysteries. For he spared no cost to win their love, providing amusements of all kinds, hunting and wine parties, and excursions to the races, till they felt towards him as to some indulgent father. 'I have seen the tears standing in their eyes,' says his biographer, 'as they recalled his memory, and fondly imitated his voice or gait, or graceful carriage.'

Others, like Adrian, pushed too far the love of finery and display. Alexander of Seleucia came to Rome on a deputation to the Emperor, and when admitted to an interview, somewhat importunately urged the prince to notice him. 'I do take notice of you,' was the reply of Antoninus, 'and I see what you are like, a coxcomb only thinking of combing your hair, cleaning your teeth, paring your nails, and scenting yourself with perfume.' We find indeed a trace of the old contrast between Philosopher and Sophist, although in altered form, when we read in the story of Alexicles, that he abandoned late in life the sage's grave and austere manners, and took to the theatre and concerts as soon as he became a Sophist.

Phil. ii. 77.

ii. 74.

Their professional gains.	They made money rapidly enough so soon as they rose to eminence, and no profession of the day brought in such incomes. Isocrates, some centuries before, though fresh from the lessons of his master Socrates, who spoke of payment as a sort of simony, had opened a school of rhetoric at Chios, afterwards at Athens, and took from 1,000 drachmæ to a talent
Phil. ii. 84.	for a course of lectures. Scopelianus in later days was still more highly paid, for he received from the young Herodes Atticus a gift of 15 talents, and the grateful father, we are told, gave him as much, and showed his admiration for him by destroying all the statues of the rival Sophists which had graced his numerous corridors.
	This was exceptional of course, as was the fortune
Phil. ii. 107.	of this princely house. But Damianus the Ephesian, who spent so much on gifts to his fellow-citizens and repairs to the great temple, paid 10,000 drachmæ at one time to both of the great teachers whom he heard. Commonly they were content with lower fees, which however mounted up to a good figure
Phil. ii. 95.	when the auditors were many. Chrestus of Byzantium, whom the Athenians tried to get elected for one of their own Chairs, had 100 paying pupils at one time. Some who had good means of their own were very moderate in their demands. Proclus of
Phil. ii. 106.	Naucratis, for example, took 100 drachmæ once for

all from each, and let him listen to as many courses as he would; out of that sum he provided even a library for the special use of his own pupils, that they might look up all the references at once, and so expand his oral teaching. He carried so far his independence, we are told, as to insist on strictest discipline. Strange to say, he would not let his pupils hiss or laugh, but made them sit quite quietly; the servants and pedagogues together on one side, and the young students marked off by themselves.

There was an important privilege attaching to the educational profession, which dates also from the Antonines. The teachers for the most were free from all taxation; at least in the smaller towns of Asia, and probably elsewhere, three Sophists and three Grammarians enjoyed immunity, while in the larger there might be five of each. The Philosophers were to be all free, but it was owned that there were few to claim the privilege. *The immunities from civil burdens enjoyed by the professors.*

This was a far greater boon in those days than it would seem at present. Civic burdens, cheerfully borne in earlier ages by the men of substance, while the currents of free life flowed strongly, were felt to be more grievous as public spirit grew more feeble, and the number of the town councillors diminished. Aristides tells us without shame in his confessions, how the local honours of all kinds pursued him, each with some heavy burden on his funds; how he wept and prayed and fasted, till at length by special favour of his guardian powers, he saw a vision of white maids who came to free him, and woke to find a letter from the Emperor, which conferred the much longed-for dispensation.

<small>Examples of imperial caprice in the treatment of the Sophists.</small>

But Imperial caprice sometimes withheld what Imperial favour had bestowed. Academic quarrels now and then were heard of by the court at Rome, and the professors were sent for in post haste to advocate their rival claim. 'No wonder if they sometimes lost heads and floundered in their speech,' <small>Phil. ii. 114.</small> says the compassionate biographer of Heraclides; 'a vulgar advocate might keep his courage up, but a professor used to lecture students may be easily unnerved at the sight of the armed body-guard, and a prince's grave look and haughty words with no encouraging applause.'

The poor Professor lost part of his salary, if not his Chair at Athens, though he does not seem to have been unmercifully badgered like Philiscus. The <small>Phil. ii. 121.</small> latter, it would seem, had gained a Professorship through influence at court, but Caracalla, whose consent had been surprised, resented the appointment, and took an early opportunity of paying off the score.

A lawsuit, in which the Professor was a party, was brought up by appeal to Rome, and the Emperor sat in judgment. As soon as Philiscus came into the hall he gave offence by his gait and carriage, and even by the way in which he wore his clothes. His voice was too falsetto, his style seemed slovenly, and there was a want of definite meaning in his words. The Emperor began to criticise him sharply, and cut him short with interruptions, confusing him with a pitiless cross-examination. The puzzled Sophist ventured to remind his master that he had once done him the honour to set him free from all taxation. Whereupon the Sovereign roared out in a passion, 'I will not have you free, nor any paltry schoolmaster like yourself. I will not rob my cities of the sources of their incomes for such miserable stuff as you can talk.'

Caracalla showed as little favour in dealing with philosophy. He fancied himself a second Alexander, and resented the coolness between Aristotle and his favourite hero, and accused the philosopher of being privy to his distinguished pupil's death. To avenge him, he disgraced all the Peripatetic doctors whom he knew, talked of burning all their books, suspended their fellowships in the Alexandrian Museum, and in his mad way discountenanced all learning. *The interests of learning suffered from the whims of Caracalla.*

But the interests of letters had far more to fear than from the wanton freaks of Caracalla. Hard times set in, and lasted nearly till the end of the third century. Anarchy and foreign war exhausted the resources of the empire. The rulers on the throne had often no breadth of views or cultivation, and the great sovereigns who restored the credit of the Roman arms upon the Northern frontiers were too busy and unlettered to prize the studious arts of peace. The endowments therefore of the Antonines were dropped; the Imperial Chairs at Athens were left vacant, though the city, to whom her University was dear, still managed to reserve some funds for the salaries of Grammarians and Sophists.

Still more in the third century from war and faction.

The older schools of Metaphysics suffered most. Longinus, the greatest schooolman of the age (the 'living library,' as Eunapius calls him) speaks of the many Philosophers whom he had known in youthful days at Athens, although he owns that, with the exception of Plotinus and his set, they all did little more than repeat and comment on the same old worn-out doctrines; 'but now,' he adds in later years, 'it is impossible to describe how entirely these studies are neglected.'

Philosophy suffered most.

Longin. ap. Porphyr. Plotin.

It is no wonder that the University declined. About this time the tide of war rolled up to Athens, and swept with furious force over her land and city.

Athens stormed by the Goths, who were, however,

The Gothic Heruli, stirred by sudden impulse from the regions of the Dniester, made their way across the Euxine, and through the Bosporus and Hellespont. The isles of Greece, the coasts of Asia, were pillaged as they passed along; and, emboldened by success, they pushed on further, and sweeping across Attica they stormed the city walls. The citizens took refuge in the woods of Parnes and Pentelicus, whence they looked with panic fear at the smoke rising from their ravaged homesteads. But one Dexippus, trained as he was in all the learning of the schools, turned his skill in rhetoric to good account by pointing to the Goths as they straggled past in careless triumph, laden with rich booty, and urging his countrymen to take courage and attack them. Emboldened by his fiery words, the fugitives poured down upon the Gothic rear, and swept them away in ignominious flight. *[routed by Dexippus]*

Brighter times at length returned with the rule of Constantine and his successors. Once more the schools of Athens filled with students; her Chairs of Rhetoric attracted the most brilliant men of letters, and the fourth century was, at least in outward seeming, the palmiest age of her ancient University. The materials for history, at any rate, are more abundant than before. The lives of the most accomplished schoolmen are written for us in the pages of Euna- *[The fourth century a brilliant age for the University of Athens, and has left more materials for history.]*

pius; the popular Libanius studied there in early years, and his writings illustrate at large the character and methods of the professional teaching which was the same at Antioch as at Athens. Himerius, who held a Chair, has left us specimens of his style; the great churchmen, Basil and Gregory Nazianzen, attended lectures there for years together by the side of the Apostate Julian, and their pictures of the scenes of student life are unusually clear and circumstantial.

Her name still exercised the same fascination as of old, and the standard of her culture was admitted on all hands to be the highest. 'Nymphidianus,' says his biographer, 'had not indeed the experience and the discipline of Athens, yet he was still worthy of the name of Sophist.' The kinsmen of the young Libanius were urgent to keep him still at Antioch; his mother wept at the thought of his departure, and friends offered him rich heiresses in marriage; but he would go, and 'would have declined the hand even of a goddess to see the smoke of Athens.' Disenchanted as he was with the lectures which he heard, yet he deeply prized his opportunities for study, and the associations of the city; he stayed there four years, and hoped to remain as many more, and says long afterwards of a friend that he was happy in his longer sojourn in the seat of learning; for his

Eunap. Nymph.

Lib. i. 11, ed. Reiske.

own part, 'he saw it but as in a dream and passed away.'

Christians even half forgave the tenacity with which it clung to the old pagan creed, and fathers sent their sons to the stronghold of heathendom, though probably with some misgivings, such as those which pious parents feel in our days when their children go amid what they fear as the temptations of free thought.

The Public Chairs were endowed partly by the central government, and partly from the city funds. The former, or what we may call the Regius Professorships, were, as before, subject to the State control; but the Emperors were too busy with nice questions of the Arian controversy, and the guidance of Church councils, to have much time or interest to spare for studies of philology and grammar; there was no Minister of Education then in office, so the Provincial Governor took, to some extent, his place. *The endowed Chairs,*

Thus we hear of a conspiracy of jealous rivals to bribe the Proconsul, and induce him to strip Proæresius of his office; at another time, when the peace of the University had been disturbed by factious spirit, we are told that the Governor of Greece drove three Professors from their Chairs, and appointed others in their stead. Nor was the State content with nominating and dismissing in such *and influence of the Provincial Governor. Eunapius Proær. Lib. i. 19.*

cases only. Edicts were put forth requiring all public teachers to be men of unblemished character; careless livers, who called themselves philosophers, were to be taken up at once and sent back to their homes; and no one was to teach except with the sanction of the Town Council, as expressed in a formal document, which was to be submitted to the Emperor.

<small>Theod. Cod. xiii. 3.</small>

<small>Liban. iii. 165.</small>

<small>Official salaries varying like tithe rent-charge.</small>

The emoluments of office took, as before, the shape of salaries, immunities and fees; but in the first an important difference was made, which it is of interest to note. From various causes the standard of value had been changing rapidly, causing great and widespread distress. Diocletian had tried, but vainly, to arrest the evil by issuing a long list of legalised prices. Such fluctuations would bear hardly on fixed incomes, as experience has proved in our days, and therefore professional stipends were either partly paid in kind, or varied with the price of corn, on the principle of tithe rent-charge.

<small>The lecture-rooms.</small>

As lecture-rooms they used sometimes a temple, or the Senate-house on great occasions; more frequently, for ordinary teaching, they remained at home: indeed, early in the century, when there had been much rioting and license in the streets, no Sophist dared to show himself abroad, but each lectured quietly in his own house; and if the students

<small>Eunap. Julian.</small>

wished to give a testimonial of more than usual value, they built a theatre, as it was called, for their Professor.

It may be noticed that we often have to read of the jealous bickerings between the rival schoolmen, and in general it must be owned that there are no traces of any bond of union between Professors, or of much corporate feeling between the members of the University. We may take the following story as an illustration of this and other features of their social life, remembering that it comes from one who knew them well, and was in full sympathy with the spirit of their institutions.

<small>Jealousies of rival Sophists</small>

<small>illustrated from Eunapius Proœr.</small>

Anatolius, the Imperial viceregent in the Illyrian provinces, was a man of great ability and cultivated tastes, and had long wished to visit Greece, to which he was attracted by so many learned memories, though himself from the legal University of Berytus. He arranged at last to take it in the course of his ministerial tour, and sent a message to the various Sophists that it was his pleasure that, when he came, they should dispute before him on a certain thesis, which he named, and that all should do their best. 'All Hellas,' says the writer, in his inflated style, 'was startled when it heard how wise and learned and incorruptible a judge was coming.' The schoolmen began to put themselves in training, and to intrigue against each other; at length they met in solemn conclave to discuss the meaning of the problem—a foolish one enough, the writer thinks it—but failed to come to an agreement, and went home, each in his vanity thinking himself right, and airing his arguments before his pupils. At last the dreaded visitor arrived, while the poor Sophists were racking their brains over the problem, and furbishing their weapons of debate. No sooner had the minister attended Divine service, and gone the round of all the temples, than he had the Convocation of the Masters summoned, and the disputations opened. They began in hot haste to display their cleverness, but failed entirely to satisfy their judge. He only laughed at their vanity for caring to be clapped by their young pupils, and pitied the parents who entrusted their children to such teachers. But at length came the turn of Proæresius, who, somewhat unfairly, had a hint of the way in which the great man liked the problem treated. So he gave such a turn to the whole argument, and treated it with such consummate elegance of style, that Anatolius started from his seat in joy, and the whole Convocation burst into applause, exclaiming that it was superhuman skill.

<small>Another illustration</small> Another scene, from the same writer, brings still more markedly before us the intensity of faction in

their midst, and the spirit of their rhetoric. Proæ-resius had been driven from Athens by bribery and intrigue; but a new Governor came to Greece, with instructions to restore him to his Chair. The exile, escorted by his friends, returned; but his enemies began to plot, 'raising their heads again like vipers full of mischief.' Meanwhile the great man made his entry into the town, and had a Convocation called, in which questions for debate were started, which the Sophists treated as they could, under cover of their friends' applause. But on a sudden, as the partisans of the banished man came in with him, the Governor spoke out: 'I intend to name a thesis, and hear you all dispute upon it then and there. Proæresius shall come last, or take his turn when you will.' The others hurriedly excused themselves, upon the plea that they were not used to speak extempore. The Governor called on Proæresius to begin. After a few graceful sentences by way of prelude, he waited to have a subject given him, and meantime began to lose his nerve, as he saw scowling faces all around him, and his friends so few. But, as it happened, at the far end of the room he espied two practised rhetoricians who had been most active in the cabal against him. By sudden impulse he begged to have them called, and put upon their oath to own that they had wronged him. They slunk away, but were recalled

from Eunapius of the bitter feeling of rivalry among the Sophists, by force, and bidden to name a theme. They did this with the worst grace 'possible, and named a barren subject, most ill-suited to rhetorical expansion. Proæresius eyed them sternly, then turning to the seat of judgment, begged earnestly that short-hand writers might come in to stand beside him. The petition granted, he further asked that no one should applaud. This too was ordered, on pain of grave displeasure. Then Proæresius let the current of his eloquence flow on, rounding each phrase with the appropriate rhythm. The hearers hardly could keep still, betraying their feelings by involuntary sounds. At length his style grew more impassioned, and leaving the poor theme suggested, as too easy for his genius, he passed on to deal with an opponent's thesis. Then, as the crowd could scarcely suppress its admiration, or the short-hand writers keep pace with his rapid course, he turned to them and said, 'Now note if I remember what was uttered; see if I fail or falter for a single word.' Then he repeated the harangue without a change of phrase or word. Thereon the Governor and assembly alike forgot the rule of silence, and broke out into acclamations. They crowded round the speaker, and kissed his hands and feet, as of a very Mercury of eloquence; even his jealous rivals could not withhold their praises. The magistrate and guards conducted him away in state.

and of their rhetorical skill.

Three Professors of this age stand out in marked prominence beyond the rest, and nearly all the Academic history of Athens connects itself for many years with one or other of their names. Julian, the earliest in date, came from Cappadocia, the country which produced some of the greatest Churchmen of the times. Proæresius, his pupil and successor in his Chair, was an Armenian by birth, and came with many of his countrymen in early life to the famous seat of learning. Hellenic letters had not long found their way into Armenia, but now they were welcomed with enthusiasm, and young men of the slenderest means set out boldly on the journey, and crowded to the schools of Athens. Gregory Nazianzen, who knew them well, gives them a bad character for truth and frankness, but notices their subtlety in dialectic. Himerius, the last great name among the Sophists, was a native of Bithynia. *The three great Sophists of the age,*

It will be seen that all these eminent teachers were Asiatic rather than Hellenic, and the other evidences of the times point to the same fact, that the old historic races were little represented at the University, and that Greek culture was then travelling further eastward, nearer to the sources of the influence, which probably in distant ages first stirred to vigorous life the civilisation of old Greece. We may find in the pages of Eunapius materials for the *rather Asiatic than Hellenic in race.*

personal history of all the three, though the details are somewhat fantastic and uncritical, and the style is full of tawdry affectations. One of them, Himerius, has also left us specimens of his orations, and there are many writings still remaining of Libanius, who, though he filled a public Chair elsewhere, had passed his student life at Athens, and represented the general spirit of her schools. Together they provide us with evidence enough of the methods and value of their professional teaching, and of their general mode of dealing with the young minds brought under their influence.

<small>The general character of their educational influence.</small>

We notice first that the personal tie was very close between the student and the lecturer, who took to some extent the place of tutor. The University was not an organized whole, which could exert a discipline through officials of its own; but each newcomer put himself at once upon a lecturer's list, and looked to him exclusively for guidance in his course of study.

<small>The personal ties between teacher and student were very close,</small>

The teacher not only marked out the student's line of reading, and admitted him to all his courses of instruction, but watched over his progress, applied encouragement or blame, visited him if he was sick, corresponded in many cases with his parents, till the bond of mutual confidence was very close and real. Indeed, the indignity was keenly felt in the case of any disruption of the tie, or desertion of the tutor by the pupil. Libanius draws a lively picture of the distress occasioned in such cases. The poor Professor finds no relish in his food or books, he cannot sleep of nights for thinking of the slight; his Chair in the lecture hall reminds him of it, and he looks with suspicious eyes upon the audience that still remains. Even more poignant is the wound if he meets his old pupil coming from another course, and sees or fancies that he is eyeing him with a bold or sneering look, or if the father storms, instead of paying what is due, and says that his son has made no progress, and ought to have left him long ago. Such apostasy —so strong is the expression of Libanius—was rare in the good old days when men used to shun the ungrateful student who treated his teacher with so little grace; but it was getting sadly common, and some were even bold enough to go the whole round of lecturers, and see which they liked best. So the tutors could not hold their own, or tighten the reins of discipline, or punish the unruly scholars; a word, a blow, was quite enough to frighten them away for ever, and swell the numbers of a rival's class. Even the pedagogues, or private tutors, conspired often to make matters worse; they took offence if their favour was not courted by fair words or fees or by good cheer, and they carried their

and desertion keenly felt by the lecturer.
ii. 423.

young charges off to a more obsequious or liberal Sophist.

So Libanius proposes to restore by mutual consent the good old custom. He would introduce a general pledge, that no teacher should accept the runaway pupil of another, but that they should drop their bitter rivalries in the sense of common good. He sees indeed the danger of this system of protection, this enforcement of the rules of a trade union of Professors, but he relies on their enthusiasm for learning, and their desire of applause to spur on the least industrious or brilliant teachers.

<small>The evils of rivalry</small>

<small>i. 313.</small>

One of the worst features of the system seemingly was the frequent bickering and strife among these jealous rivals. Libanius, indeed, takes credit to himself for patience, when he hears of the bearded men who go to listen to another lecturer; but he fumes as much as anyone when a youth deserts his class, and he is full of bitterness against his colleagues.

<small>avoided sometimes by special unions,
ii. 812.</small>

Sometimes it would seem that such collision was avoided by special unions or systems of gradation, in which one took higher rank than all the rest.

We are hearing in our own days of plans of organizing study, by which provision may be made for each department by Professors with the help of deputies or readers, but it is not easy to determine the relations in such cases. The picture given in Libanius is curious, but not attractive. In one such group, in which a Professor from Ascalon was 'Coryphæus of the Choir,' 'when the head appeared, the others rose in haste, and hurried to escort him to his Chair, and waited for his nod before they took their seats; they dared not look him in the face, but bowed their head to show their reverence, and all the time that he was present, they dared not think of anything save what he said.' This was not all. When the other lecturers were paid, his servant came to claim his toll for all that they received. Three such 'choirs' we read of in Libanius, but we know little of the nature of their harmony, nor, indeed, whether it was by arrangement of their own, or as an institution of the State that they existed. The Professors had to entertain each other, we are told, at dinner at stated times, as a sort of Tutors' Club, in forms prescribed by custom, if not by law, besides all that was left to the free hospitality of each.

Libanius himself was quite a professional magnate, and took high rank in the scholastic world, mingling on equal terms with civic dignitaries and imperial ministers, nor scrupling now and then to pour out the vials of his wrath upon them when he felt himself slighted or aggrieved. But he was a servant of the State himself, and could be called to account for his official work. It is curious to read his answer to one critic who accused him of neglect of duty. The lecturer and his class had been listening one morning to an essay written by a promising young pupil, for each in turn wrote out and read some sort of exercise in public, as a kind of 'Terminal Collections.' On such occasions there was no other lecture given in the course of the forenoon, and the Professor was chatting with his friends, when up came a private tutor, protesting, in the interest of his young charge, against the many holidays which were allowed. 'Here was a day wasted in listening to a theme from a young prentice hand; at other times they had to sit in idleness while the Sophists showed their vanity in speeches of parade, and then the teacher often missed his lectures on the plea that he was ill, or had to attend on the funeral of some acquaintance; and even when the class was kept to study, they spent so much time over the old classics, that they never seemed to be getting forward with the real work of education.' It is needless to inquire into the justice of these personal attacks, or follow the accused in his defence; it is enough to see that in the Universities of old such charges might be made, and must be met.

but was sharply called to account for his professional work. ii. 266.

The holidays at any rate were getting fewer. At Antioch, we read, the fasts and feasts, or Saints' days,

Lib. i. 237.

as we may call them, were still marked upon the calendar, but respect for them was growing feeble.

The Professor sent, it seems, on one of them, to bid his class attend his lecture, but they all declined to come on the plea of tender conscience, or some mysterious presentiment of evil that might follow. One pupil only appeared upon the scene, and brought an essay with him for correction, which they began to read together. They had not gone on long, however, when a mass of stone and rubbish came tumbling from the roof, nearly burying the student and Professor, and bearing witness to the anger of the slighted Saint, to whom the lecturer addresses a sort of elaborate apology, by writing for the public a history of the event. Such penal consequences have not followed yet perhaps from the like violation of old customs in our midst.

It was with natural pride that the great Sophists pointed to the proof of their world-wide reputation in the numbers who streamed to them from every land. Libanius, in one of his orations, replying to an imaginary critic, says that he is too modest to aver that he has filled the three continents and all the islands, as far as the pillars of Hercules, with rhetoricians, but that he certainly has spiritual children—for so he likes to call them—in Thrace, Constantinople, and Bithynia, in the Hellespont,

The Sophists' pride in the number of their pupils.

iii. 444.

Ionia, and Caria; some few even among the Paphlagonians and Cappadocians. Far more there were in Galatia and in Armenia, and most of all in Cilicia and Syria. 'If you cross the Euphrates, and visit the cities which lie beyond it, you will find some not unworthy members of our brotherhood. Phœnicia besides, and Palestine, and Arabia owe me some gratitude.'

Among the remaining speeches of Himerius are several addressed to the freshmen who had lately joined his classes. He is careful in every case to note their birth-place, and to add some flattering words of reference to the historic glories or the present importance of their race, while dwelling on his pleasure at being brought into such wide-spread relations. But he does not forget to respect his dignity amid such complimentary phrases, and to magnify the importance of his office. The language of his opening address is as solemn as that of any priest of the Eleusinian rites. They are grave mysteries, of which he holds the keys, and the process of initiation has begun. 'Before the ceremony opens which is to give you access to the sanctuary, let me distinctly warn you what you should do, and what refrain from. Let the ball drop from your hands, and the pen alone engage your care; the sports of the gymnasium must cease, and the studio

The language of Himerius to the freshmen was

as solemn as that of a priest at the mysteries. Him. ed. Wernsdorf. xxii. 7.

of the Muses be thrown open. Delicate or wanton habits ill accord with industry; come to me, if you will, unwashed, so you set your foot on self-indulgence. There in a few words you have my precepts and my rule. The obedient hearer shall find grace and light. The careless and refractory shall be warned off the holy fire, and find no access to the sanctuary of eloquence. The warning applies indeed to all, but specially to you who are freshmen but of yesterday.'

There followed a sort of introduction of the younger to the senior students, in which the same set of religious images recurs, drawn from the language of the mysteries. 'The adept already familiar *xv. 3.* with the sacred way is the best guide to initiate the inexperienced novice, as old sailors can best steer the ship, and old hounds teach the young ones how to hunt.'

Then began in the forenoon a systematic course of study, for later in the day private lectures only were given for older men who had a taste for learning. The young students read and commented together on the writings of the classics, on the older authors, that is, whose style seemed purest or sentiments the noblest. Thus, in Libanius we have a scholar complaining to himself, 'What shall I gain from all this ceaseless work, in which I have to read right through so many poets, and so many rhetoricians, and writers of every style of composition?' The lecturers discoursed on the beauties, or on the characteristic features, of the authors; while the students, assisted sometimes by the slaves who wrote short-hand, took down the notes of what they heard, to reproduce it on occasion. It would seem that they were diligent enough in this respect, as in our own day, for we read that in a single month they filled their note-books many times with hints and illustrations of good style. The comments were often wearisomely long, if we may trust a critic, who talks of their 'wasting as much time in dissecting one poor book as the Greek warriors spent at Troy.' Their studies in philology extended only to one language. The literature of Rome was quite ignored by these disdainful schoolmen, as unworthy to be mentioned by the side of Demosthenes and Homer. Even Demosthenes himself seemed somewhat too bare and unadorned in style to suit the fastidious taste of this late age; he was read and quoted with respect, indeed, but the real models of their imitation were the showy and inflated periods of masters of rhetoric like Polemon and Aristides. Meantime they laid to heart elaborate theories of literary grace; trained their ears to catch the rhythm of each sentence, and to note the significance of accent, and the varying use of anapæst or spondee at the close of every

[margin: Libanius, ii. 293. Themistius, 289a. Libanius, ii. 273. but only of the Greek language, together with rules of rhetoric.]

period. Verbal analysis was not forgotten; rules of synonyms and homonyms and paronyms had to be mastered and remembered, with all the machinery of tropes and figures.

Before long the principles must be applied to compositions of their own, and essays and themes of every kind became the order of the day. The pedagogues might lend their aid, and recall to memory the lecturer's hints, turn out the classical authors whose thoughts or images could be pressed into the service, or stimulate the flagging industry of their young charges. But the exercises must be brought in time under the Professor's eye, to be examined and corrected, and to serve as evidence of progress made. Their fluency of speech was trained meantime, and all the rules of dialectic learnt. It was not enough for them to bring their essays carefully prepared on subjects long ago suggested; they must learn to improvise on any question laid before them, show their perfect self-possession and easy grace in an extempore debate. *Original compositions were required, and exercises in logic and elocution*

They stored their memories for this purpose with a whole stock of common-places (χρείαι) which could readily be turned to good account; they studied their teacher's oratorical displays, which were published often for their use, that they too might learn to show off upon occasion with an elaborate harangue (ἐπίδειξις). They fancied themselves bidding adieu to friends upon a journey, and took leave in appropriate style (προπεμπτικοὶ λόγοι); or addressed complimentary speeches (προσφωνηματικοί) to the great men, ministers of state or generals, who might one day look in upon them at their work. Or they took their themes from ancient history, and declaimed, like the Roman lads of Juvenal's age, and gave their good advice to Sulla, or wrangled about the course of action which it would have been wiser for Hannibal to follow.

But the Sophists professed to aim at far more than rhetoric.
Greg. in laud. Basil.

The lecturers were very far indeed from saying that their pupils needed only to have courses of rhetoric and logic. Their curriculum of study had a much more ambitious sound. Thus Gregory Nazianzen tells us that his friend Basil, little as he was in sympathy with the spirit of the place, traversed the whole round of academic study, not only mastered rhetoric and philology, but excelled all others in philosophy, including in the term ethics and metaphysics, as well as the rules of dialectic. Not content with that, he went on to mathematical inquiries, rising even to astronomy, after learning the properties of numbers and of figures. Then at last he studied medicine, both in theory and practice.

So too, when Himerius traces a sketch of the liberal education of his day in the person of his friend

Hermogenes, he made him speedily devote himself to the study of philosophy, in the several stages of morals, physics and theology. In so doing he mastered not merely the doctrines of a single school, but was at home alike in all the great systems of Greek thought. Like Basil, he too learnt astronomy, and also travelled far and wide to gain a practical acquaintance with the outer face of nature.

But, indeed, we need not be so much impressed with this encyclopædia of learning. With all their imposing names these sciences were something quite different from what we think them now. The experimental methods had not been applied as yet, and few of nature's secrets were discovered, as compared with the stores of information since amassed. *But the course of study was more imposing than profound.*

In place of careful study of the facts, men accepted principles unproven, oftentimes unprovable; they dealt with theories instead of things; and speculation in all the spheres of philosophy, morals, and religion tended to mystic reverie and edifying talk. In the academic schools, moreover, such grave studies were not pursued from any earnest love of truth, from the real desire to probe the mysteries of nature, or draw the veil a little further back; but rather as a source of varied illustration, to furnish the rhetorician's stock-in-trade, to give a glib assurance to the speaker, or a show of dignified omniscience.

Armed with a large array of sounding phrases, and passing with ease from technicalities to commonplace, he could suit himself to every hearer, and hold his own on every question in debate.

<small>The evidence remaining in the public lectures of distinguished professors;</small>

Is such a criticism thought too sweeping or severe? We may turn, perhaps with interest, to see how far it is confirmed by the works which have come down to us from the masters of the schools. These are, as it is natural to suppose, their greater efforts: inaugural addresses at the opening of term, when the holidays of summer had passed by, and the lecturer met his class again. Often they were lectures of parade, delivered in the Long Vacation, when the daily catechisings were suspended, and time and energy were left entire for bolder flight of rhetoric. Or when distinguished visitors passed by, crowned heads, or ministers, or provincial governors, and the local magistrates came out in state to do them honour, the ceremony was not thought complete if the foremost orator did not grace it with a speech.

<small>as, for example, of Himerius.</small>

For purposes like these the talents of Himerius were always in request. An encomium or elegy from his pen was looked for as a thing of course on state occasions, as much as in later days an ode from a Poet Laureate, or an *éloge* from a French Academician. Take all, or any of these lectures—there are some volumes ready for our use by different authors—read and re-read in search of the ripe fruit of all this varied study. Where are the new canons of literary taste, the fine theories of poetic art, the principles of historic method, the critical survey of great schools of moral thought. Now, if ever, surely might a large and learned eclecticism flourish, comparing and balancing the errors of one-sided systems, full of delicate sympathy and insight, if wanting in creative power. We turn over the pages, and we only feel the more how impossible it is to enter fully into the thoughts and feelings of the generations that are gone. We know that the charms of style are evanescent, and we must lose the graces of natural gesture and of modulated voice; but surely here is a poor outcome of all this earnest study, and all this gathered store of learning, in thought which hardly ever rises above the sameness of dull common-place, relieved but ill by tags of poetry and borrowed images, which to our modern taste seem often incongruous and insipid.

It may be urged, indeed, and with some show of reason, that we have here only the works of rhetoricians, more intent on beauty of form than breadth of thought, and that for the higher education of the age we must turn to other teachers. It may be well to weigh both these objections. As to the first, it is quite true that there is a real danger of injustice in

It is hard, indeed, for us to do justice to the rhetorical beauties of Greek style.

our criticism of these schoolmen. It is so hopeless for us now to try to feel what the sensitive ears of the old Greeks must have felt, we are so ignorant of the rhythmical melodies of the language which they spoke, and whose resources they studied with so fond a love, that periods which roused them to enthusiasm fall flat and cold on our unsympathetic nerves. Nor is this all, our sensibilities for grace and beauty have certainly not kept pace with our scientific progress. Our deepest thinkers are often quite indifferent to the elegance of literary form. They may see to it that the words shall faithfully reflect the thoughts, but beyond that they often neglect entirely the niceties of style, and would almost despise themselves for caring much about the harmonies of balanced cadence, or the subtleties of characteristic phrase. And so we listen with a natural impatience when we hear of the laboured efforts of these rhetoricians to gain an entire mastery over the beauties of their language, or to make perfection of the outward form their end and aim. Yet after all they were musicians, playing on an instrument of many strings; and if through them they stirred the fancy and touched the hearts of a thousand hearers, we have no right to underrate their skill, because some of the strings are tuneless in our ears, or our ignorant hands have never learnt to use them deftly.

But is it true, that at the University there was much teaching of a higher order, thrown into the shade, perhaps, by the popular graces of these literary artists, but still ready, if required, for any deep and earnest thinkers? One potent influence of this kind there was elsewhere already, soon to be better represented also in the schools of Athens, for without doubt the Neoplatonic system was not wanting in vigour or intensity of thought. But we cannot take this as the type of what was then in vogue, as the professorial teaching of philosophy. Rather for that purpose we may take Themistius, versed in all the Aristotelian lore, and famous at this time as Public Lecturer in the New Rome, the seat of Empire. A volume of his popular works survives to show us what was the spirit of his teaching. He is very careful, more than once, to hold himself distinct from all the Sophists of the day. To make the contrast more explicit, he describes them as Plato did his rivals of old time, following closely in his master's steps, and using the same definitions for the heads of his own lecture. Thanks to his own ample means, he need not teach in any mercenary spirit, or vex his pupils for their tutor's dues, or, like his rivals, puff and advertise his literary wares; but thanks still more to the genial spirit of philosophy, he was raised above suspicion of betraying the interests of truth,

Was there much teaching of a higher order?

The celebrated Themistius, though professedly a philosopher, and making the worse appear the better cause. The Sophists might dwell contentedly in their unrealities of dreamland, but eternal verities alone engaged the attention of his class.

If so, however, it must be admitted that only the privileged few might enter into the inner circle of such mysteries. In the discourses which are left, he has borrowed all the rhetorician's tools, and used them seemingly without misgiving. Homeric illustrations cropping up in subjects most incongruous to their use, frigid conceits of stalest imagery, wordy developments of thought already worn threadbare, this is what Themistius thought enough to attract an ignorant public to the fruits of liberal culture.

is as popular and rhetorical in his lectures as the Sophists.

He takes credit to himself for forming the character of those who listen, and helping them forward on the road to virtue; and indeed his lectures read often like dull sermons, though delivered from the Professor's Chair. But as preachers of righteousness the schoolmen were easily surpassed by the great doctors of the church, who like themselves had mastered all the rules of rhetoric, and used them in a nobler cause. Some there were, indeed, who tried to breathe new life into the dry bones of heathen ethics, whose mystic enthusiasm and devotional warmth were quite unknown to earlier ages; but they could not vie with the fire of intense conviction,

As moral preachers, he and the Sophists were easily surpassed by the Christian doctors.

the vigour of invective, the weight of personal character with which their rivals denounced the vices of the age, or enlarged upon the mysteries of faith.

In another chapter we may enter more into details upon the struggle between the old and new religions, in so far as it affects the subject now before us; it remains only here to note its influence on the outer fortunes of the schools, in their fading prestige and dwindling numbers. We may fail, indeed, to recognise the change, so long as we are only dealing with the greatest names among the schoolmen. We see that they still take a high rank in their cities, have honours and riches showered upon them, receive distinctions from their Sovereigns, and even military decorations, as Proæresius was made the colonel of a regiment, and had a statue raised to him at Rome, with the inscription on it, 'the Queen of Cities to the King of Eloquence.' They are indispensable on state occasions, as the official orators of every important cause. Provincial Governors send them pupils as a mark of their esteem, and go in state to their inaugural addresses. Sometimes also they honour them by letting their own children join the class, forgetting however to send the customary fees, or even any present of fruit, or wine, or game. *[margin: This may partly account for the dwindling numbers and reputation of the schools. Eunapius Proær. Libanius, iii. 134.]*

But the rank and file are not so lucky, and before long they keenly feel the suspense and discouragement of a decaying trade. We have, indeed, a humorous definition of the Sophist, given us by one of their own number, in which stress is laid on their big houses, multitudes of pupils, rounded paunch, and insinuating ways. But the reverse of the picture is presented, though still in jesting vein, by the same writer, when he maintains that the Sophist's trade is but a form of slavery, in gilded chains at best. He has to flatter the friends and parents of his pupils, and say that they are prodigies of talent, though they may be hopeless blockheads; he must pay court to the innkeepers and tradesmen, and the masters of the lodging-houses, that they may not give him a bad name, or prejudice the freshmen against his training-college for young sophists (σοφιστῶν ἐργαστήριον); he must make interest with the Aldermen, lest in a fit of spleen or of caprice they may deprive him of his Chair; he must not even forget to have a ready word and liberal fee for the porters at the great men's houses. When the day comes for any of his studied lectures, to which the general public is invited, the veriest dolt, the most irreverent witling, soldier or pugilist or what-not, may spoil his happiness by checking the natural movement of applause. The writer however does not always speak so lightly. One of his speeches contains a strong appeal in behalf of the poorer members of his own profession, in which he

[marginalia: Liban. Epist. 401.; ii. 79.]

draws a melancholy picture of the misery to which they were exposed. A French bishop pleading for his clergy, who can scarcely live upon their scanty pittance, taunting the state for its cruel neglect of so many of its faithful servants; this would be, perhaps, the nearest analogue in our experience to the Sophist's expostulation with the citizens of Antioch. 'Be not misled,' he says, 'by names like those of orators and professorial Chairs, but listen to the truth from one who knows it well. Some of them have not even now a cottage of their own, but, like cobblers, live in hired lodgings; or if any one has bought a little house, it is still so mortgaged that the owner has more anxiety than if he had never bought it.

Illustration from a speech of Libanius on the poverty of the professors.

Lib. ii. 209.

'One has three slaves, another two, a third still fewer; these are all the more insolent and tipsy, because their master is so poor.... One rhetorician counts himself a lucky man because he only has a single child; another thinks his numerous family a real misfortune; the prudent avoid marriage altogether. In former days, the schoolmen used to stroll into the goldsmiths' shops, and talk freely to the craftsmen, finding fault with the workmanship of one, or pointing out the finer tooling, or praising them for promptitude, or blaming them if they were too slow. Now they have to deal mainly with the bakers, to whom they owe the very bread they eat;

they have to promise that they soon will pay, and beg a little more meantime; they are driven to grievous straits, for they would gladly shun their shops, because they are ashamed to owe them money, but are forced by hunger to go to them again. As the debt goes on increasing always, and no funds come in to meet it, they curse their literary craft, and carry to the bakers the earrings or necklace of their wives; they must not think what present they can give them to replace it, but only what other ornament there is to sell.

'Their lessons over, they do not hurry home, as would be natural, to enjoy their leisure, but linger awhile longer in their lecture rooms, because they know that they will feel their misery more at home. They sit down, and talk and bemoan their wretchedness to one another, but each finds that however piteous his tale, he has something worse to hear.'

The Speaker claims his right to raise his voice in their behalf even in the council chamber. Their influence had made Antioch what it was—the home of liberal studies; their moral character was worthy of themselves and of the reputation of the State. He could point to their bearing their poverty with unrepining patience, mingling with noblemen and squires, but saying nothing of their personal wants, and meantime neglecting none of the duties of their calling. The artisans, in their workshops, might indeed make much ado about the fees and presents on which the teachers grew so fat, but in sad earnest they were very few, and national help was needed if they would not see them starve.

He does not ask, however, for a grant of public money, the pressure of which would fall upon the rates; but there were waste lands at the disposal of the city, ground at least which was unclaimed at present, most of which, indeed, must go to the landowners, to meet the growing burdens of taxation, but of which, perhaps, some little might be spared to supply each teacher with a modest glebe.

It will be noticed that our information on this point deals solely with the state of things at Antioch, but the same forces were at work elsewhere, and there is reason to believe that the like holds good for Athens.

CHAPTER IV.

STUDENT LIFE.

<small>Our pictures of student life at Athens are drawn mainly from writers of the fourth century.</small> IT is from the writers of the fourth century that we mainly learn the habits of the student world at Athens. So many men of eminence, both Christians and Pagans, passed years of their growing manhood in its schools, that it is no wonder if in later life they recurred fondly to the friendships formed, the knowledge learnt, and even to the frivolities and pranks witnessed if not indulged in by themselves.

<small>Few students were of Attic race.</small> Scarcely any of the teachers, and few seemingly among the students, were of the Attic race. 'Men of all the nations subject to the Roman sway,' says Eunapius, 'were gathered there;' but the West was little represented. Italian names seldom occur in our authorities, for Autun (Augustodunum) and Trèves (Augusta Treverorum), Marseilles and Alexandria, in addition to the old imperial city, carried off probably the studious youth of one-half of the empire. But the Hellenized inhabitants of Asia Minor, and the populations of Syria and Phœnicia

betook themselves especially to Athens, whose name stood highest wherever the language and art of Greece were prized. Many came in riper years, after a long course of study, spent in one or more of the other seats of learning, as German students in our own days pass from one University to another, attracted by some celebrated name. Thus the future Emperor Julian was twenty-four, Basil was twenty-five, and Gregory Nazianzen nearly thirty when they still carried on the life which brought them there together. Sometimes even practised teachers sought to profit for a time by the experience and skill of a more conspicuous talent. But more often they were younger than the undergraduates of our own days. Eunapius the biographer was only sixteen, as he tells us, when he entered, and they are spoken of so often as mere lads in the speeches of the time that we cannot doubt that they were very young.

Some were of ripe age,

but commonly they were very young,

As they came at such an early age from distant homes, and their parents very rarely could be with them—though we do hear of some at times—they often had their personal attendants, pedagogues or private tutors, to exercise some control, and represent the influence of home. 'Watchmen and guardians,' as they were termed in the rhetorical phrases of the day; 'bulwarks to protect the growing manhood, barking hounds to frighten

who had private tutors with them;

away wolves,' they watched over the daily life of their young charges, kept them to their hours of study, warning, encouraging, and threatening even in the last resort; they travelled with them over the subject of the Professors' lectures, looked to see if their notes were rightly taken, and helped them often in their exercises. Yet they were commonly of lower social rank, and as such had not always moral weight, and even were at times exposed, as we shall see, to sorry treatment. So the public teachers were expected to exert a pastoral care; the lecturers speak of themselves as shepherds, and their audience as a flock which they must tend.

It was the first thing for every youth on his arrival to put himself upon the list of some Professor, chosen at the wish of guardians or friends, and, after some sort of examination and settlement of money terms, his name was entered on the roll, and he was made free of all the future courses. But this was not always such a simple matter as it may seem to us at first sight. Let us hear what Gregory Nazianzen has to tell us. 'Most of the young enthusiasts for learning, noble and lowborn alike, become mad partisans of their Professor. As those who have a passionate love of racing hardly can contain themselves, but copy all the gestures of the jockeys, or bet upon the horses entered for the prize, although they hardly have the wherewithal to live themselves; so the students show like eagerness for their teachers and the masters of their favourite studies: they are all anxiety to get their audience larger, and to have their fees increased. And this is carried to portentous lengths. They post themselves over the city, on the highways, about the harbour, on the tops of the hills, nay, in lonely spots; they win over the inhabitants to join their faction. As each new comer disembarks, he falls into their hands; they carry him off at once to the house of some countryman or friend, who is bent on trumpeting the praises of his own Professor, and by that means gaining his favour or exemption from his fees.'

Libanius was one of those who suffered most hardly from this practice, and in his memoirs he draws a lively picture of his treatment. Hardly had he set foot in the city, after the hazards of a winter voyage from Constantinople, than he fell into the hands of a party of these touters, who, carrying him off by main force, kept him in durance vile until he promised to give up his former plans, and attach himself to the lecturer for whom they catered. They made light of all his protests, and only let him out when he had bound himself by solemn oath. He went accordingly to lecture with them, but, whether

Libanius suffered from this practice. i. 13.

from chagrin or not, he was very painfully impressed by the feebleness of the instruction given, and was in no mood to join the others in their rapturous applause. Their scowling looks, however, speedily convinced him that it might be dangerous to criticise too freely, so he excused himself upon the plea that he was suffering from sore throat, and must sit by in silent admiration. But as soon as he safely could, he quietly gave up attending, betook himself to lonely studies, training himself on the old models, yet never quite forgot his disappointment, or spoke otherwise than with contempt of the lecturers of Athens.

<small>*The practical jokes to which the freshmen were subjected.*</small>

Nor was this the only ordeal which the freshmen had to bear. They were exposed to other treatment, in sorry taste as it may seem to us, as practical jokes are commonly, with little Attic salt about them. Yet Gregory, even in a funeral speech on his friend Basil, lingers complaisantly on such memories of their youth. He tells us how the novice, just arrived and carried off to the house of some acquaintance, was set upon and badgered by the senior men about him. If he was very fresh, and inexperienced in repartee, they resorted to mere vulgar banter; but if he showed any quickness in retort, they tried upon him all the resources of their practised wit. Wearied of this, at last they set off for a walk, which proved to be a sort of mock parade of the new-comer. Two and two they paced the streets in slow procession, till they brought him to the bath; but as they drew near they broke out suddenly into frantic uproar, as if the door were barred and they must needs take the place by storm. After this feint of assault and of defence, when the nerve of the freshman had been tested, they took him in at last, and the trials of the novitiate were over.

Now and then, by special favour, some were spared. Eunapius, on his way by sea to the Piræus, had been struck down by fever, and carried to a lodging in an almost hopeless state. A quack doctor was allowed to try his hand upon him, when his life was now despaired of, and, to the surprise of all, he cured his patient. The news spread through the city, and Prœresius, the professor, showed a lively interest when he heard it. So, turning to his class, he said, 'Excuse him, if you love me, the ordeal of the bath, and be sparing of your jests and banter; treat him as if he were my son.' *Few were spared like Eunapius*

In like manner, in the case of Basil, Gregory interceded for his countryman, whose character, he knew, was far too earnest and reserved to enter readily into such poor jests. 'This,' says Gregory, 'was the beginning of our friendship, for no one in our time, save him, was exempted from the general *and Basil.*

law.' Yet even so he did not quite escape from captious quibbles. Some Armenian students, jealous possibly of the young freshman's reputation, set upon him unawares, and tried to draw him into a dispute; and even Gregory at first failed to see their malice. But they found their match in the clear-headed Basil, who was too strong for them in dialectic, and made his way out of their snares.

<small>National differences seem to have been marked by social clubs.</small>

Besides the references already made to the ties of race among the youths, there seems evidence of closer union among the several nations represented than can be found at earlier times. In Philostratus, indeed, we read of the Greek set, as if it were kept separate from the rest; but now we are told of national differences, so strongly marked, as if they had some organised form of clubs or social unions among them, somewhat as in later days we read in modern Universities of standing jealousies between north and south, or recognised subdivision into nations. There

<small>Olympiodorus ap. Phot. 63. Lib. ii. 432.</small>

are some data even which may lead us to infer that not only were the students to be distinguished as *gownsmen* from the world, but that each nation had its own variety of academic garb. They grouped themselves in this way round their favourite Professors, attracted often by such local ties, and thus intensified by sympathies of race the passionate spirit of their partisanship.

On one occasion we are told that the whole University was split up into angry factions in the interest of rival teachers. But Proæresius had by far the largest following. All Pontus and Bithynia grouped itself around him. The western coast of Asia, from Lydia to Tarsus, was with him to a man. Even Egypt and the regions far beyond to unknown distances flocked to hear him and to sound his praises. So hot grew the disputes at times among them, that the teachers hardly dared to show themselves outside their doors, and lectured in their houses, lest their appearance in the streets, escorted home by their young partisans, should be the signal for a riot. One such we hear of more at length in the pages of Eunapius, and it may serve to illustrate still further the relation of tutor to his pupils. *The factious spirit of these illustrated by Eunapius Proær.*

Julian, the leading Sophist of his time, in the early part of the fourth century, had kept himself carefully in doors, and taught his scholars in his theatre, for fear of an affray; but some of them were set upon by students of the rival faction of Apsines, who, not content with such rough usage, actually cited them before a court of law, as if the others were the aggressors.

The case was brought for hearing before the Provincial Governor himself, who had Julian apprehended, with all his pupils who were concerned in the affair. Apsines too was present to advise and prompt his friends the prosecutors, though the Judge eyed him sternly, and asked him what business he had there. In came the accused, in bonds and piteous plight, while their Professor, dressed in mourning, stood beside them. The counsel for the prosecution then began, but the Magistrate soon cut him short, and bade the accuser state his case in his own words. But he stood stammering and confused, for he and his friends only came prepared to hiss and clamour down the speaker on the other side. As they kept silence, Julian humbly begged to be allowed to say a word. 'No one of you doctors,' said the Judge, 'shall have a chance of letting off the speeches you came primed with, nor shall any of your scholars clap you. The prosecutor shall open his case first, then, Julian, do you name any of your pupils whom you like to plead in your defence, and let him do his best.' The accuser was dumbfounded still, and the laughing-stock of all the court. Julian therefore humbly pointed to his pupil Proæresius, and asked to have him set free from his bonds, engaging that he at least should find his voice. Proæresius was brought forward, and encouraged by his master, as athletes by their friends on their entering the lists. He prefaced his speech with a few touching words of complaint at his own sorry plight, and of respectful reference to his teacher, hinting even that the Judge was acting harshly in letting him be dealt with so ignominiously when nothing had been proved against him. The Magistrate bowed his head to hide his mingled feelings of shame and of surprise, so skilfully was the rebuke administered, and so graceful was the style. The speaker then continued; but scarcely had he spoken a few words, when the Judge bounded like a young enthusiast from his chair, and shook his robe of State with loud applause, while even the Professor of the rival faction forgot his enmity in admiration.

After this story it is curious to turn to the memoirs of Libanius, and read his account of the impression made upon his young imagination by such tales of student life as made their way to him at Antioch. 'When I heard of the fighting in the streets of Athens, of the clubs and stones and the cold steel, of the wounds given and received, of the prosecutions and defence in courts of law, and of all the perils endured by the young men for the honour of their teachers, I thought as highly of their courage in facing danger as if they were fighting for their fatherland. I prayed to Heaven that I too might one day signalise myself in this way, hurrying to the Piræus or to Sunium, to carry off the novices as soon as they had landed.' Yet he was soon disenchanted with the vulgar facts, and thought the

Effect of such stories of students' brawls on the imagination of the young Libanius. i. 16.

poor Professors whom he heard quite unworthy of such self-devotion, and thanked his guardian angel that he was saved from all such risks. But strange to say, in later years, long after he had filled a public Chair himself, he could not help recurring to such brawls as a proof of the affection of the scholars for their teachers. He even taunts his pupils with the sights that he had seen elsewhere; 'wounds on the head and face and hands, wounds everywhere, sure evidence of the love they bore their tutors, as great as for their parents. But you,' he adds disdainfully, 'what service of this sort in my behalf can any of you point to? What risk or blow encountered, or what bold word or look? Nay, far from that, you run away to other teachers, taking your fees with you, and so rob one Professor, while you pay court to another.' It is not easy to imagine a state of feeling so unlike our own, or to realise the possibility of such complaints made gravely from a Professorial Chair.

Marginalia: Yet he taunts his pupils in later years for not fighting for him. i. 203.

We light upon a more familiar feature when we find that the riots of the students were not always the mere contests of rival factions; even in those days there were town and gown disorders, in which, unlike our later times, the gownsmen were most often the aggressors, breaking even into the houses of the citizens, and maltreating those they found within.

Marginalia: Town and gown riots.

As usually in ancient cities, the police force was inefficient, and the Governor had at times to interfere, and to punish the offenders. He had probably good reason for thinking that the teachers were in fault, or as Libanius puts it, 'he chastised the shepherds when the sheep ran wild.' The lecturer therefore does not fail to press good advice on his young friends. They should indeed be models of courteous amenity, charming the unlettered townsmen by the beauty of their manners, not forsaking the soft dalliance with the Muses for the rude logic of rough words and broken heads, not bandying abuses with carpenters and cobblers, nor forgetting all at once the sobering influence of the daily service in the temples. *Lib. iii. 254.*

There was besides another class which suffered now and then from the wild frolics of the wanton youth. A lecture of Libanius brings a scene before our fancy, in which a poor pedagogue is tossed in a blanket by some students who resented an act of seeming disrespect. A Proctor or Dean of later days, if the offence were brought before him, would administer rebuke or penalty in a few moments. But we realize more easily the wordy spirit of that age, when we find that the Professor writes, delivers, publishes a lengthy speech to his class among which were the offenders, drawing a *At'acks upon the pedagogues or private tutors. iii. 252.*

moving picture of the poor sufferer's fright, his present ignominy, his future shame, his hopelessness of like employment, together with the fatal blow struck at all moral discipline. He even makes a personal appeal to their good feeling, reminding them how much his own credit suffers by their bad behaviour, how unwilling parents would be to entrust their sons to one whose authority had been weakened by such flagrant outrage.

No discipline or control exerted by University authorities at Athens,

The University as such could exert no form of discipline; for there was no bond of union between the Masters; no power seemingly of legislation or of penalty; it was left to the several teachers to use such influence as they chose or could enforce; and only by sinking mutual jealousies could they come to an understanding on their common interest, or agree to a joint course of action, such as that which was proposed to check the vagrant humour of the students who would stray from one Chair to another.

or by city police,

The city on its side was afraid to alienate the students; in itself it was a petty town, with decaying trade and dwindling population; it lay no longer on the great highway of policy and commerce, and but for its University might be forgotten. So the young scholars lived as and where they pleased.

or delegates.

There were no Delegates of lodging houses to interpose between the citizen and scholar, to insist that outward decencies should be observed, and inquiries into character be made. The civil power only interfered when the heavy hand of law was needed to avenge a flagrant breach of peace.

But the State was not always so easy going in the matter. It is curious to turn from Athens and contrast the edict of Valentinian at Rome. It ran as follows:—' All who come to Rome to study must appear at once before the public registrar, and present their passports from the Justices of the peace who have given them leave to travel, that thus entry may be made of their birthplace, rank, and character. They must also on their first appearance name the faculty in which they wish to study. The Registry must also take note where they lodge, and see if they adhere to the profession they have chosen. Its officers must look to it that they all behave well in society, being careful of their good name and of the company they keep, not going to the theatre too often, nor sallying out to wine parties at a late hour of the night. Furthermore, if any one's behaviour shall have been discreditable to the interests of learning, we hereby give our Ministers authority to whip the offender publicly, and put him on shipboard at once, and send him home without delay. But those who work steadily at their professional studies may be allowed to stay at Rome till they have reached

Very different provisions at Rome.

Cod. Theod. xiv. 9.

their twentieth year.' Such rigour may perhaps have suited the stern genius of Rome, but the traditions of Athenian freedom still guarded the spirit of her studies. If we pay in fancy a visit to the lecture hall, we shall carry away probably a like impression.

The students at lecture.

The young men went, as we have seen, to the house of their Professor, attended often by their private tutors, and sometimes by a servant with their books, or even by a shorthand writer. The lectures were mostly in the morning hours, as with ourselves, at any rate for ordinary courses, for there were some others later in the day, which were different

Lib. ii. 316. in their character, attended by men of riper years, by merchants, and even soldiers it would seem who were attracted by the fence of words. They brought with them their themes to be corrected, or they took notes of the arguments and illustrations, or they were catechised on points of literary criticism, or they disputed in his presence to train themselves in readiness of speech. When the Professor spoke, they made no scruple in applauding, and the practice may surprise us less when we remember that the like was done by the congregations in the churches while listening to a sermon.

Their behaviour very bad at times, as illustrated

But their behaviour was not always so flattering to the teacher. Libanius paints a most unfavourable picture of the manners of his pupils, and though the scene in that case was at Antioch, we may well believe that the like went on at Athens. 'I send my servant out to all my scholars to summon them to lecture, and he starts off at a run to do my bidding. But they are in no mood, like him, to hurry, though they ought to be even more in haste. They stay some of them to sing their hymns, which we have all heard till we are tired, or else they amuse themselves with foolish merriment and jesting. If their friends or bystanders remark on their delay, and at last they make their mind up to be off, they talk about their sweethearts as they go, or on the skill of some dancer at the circus, and they gossip even when they get inside, to the annoyance of real students. This they do till the lecture has begun. And even when the subject is discussed, and explanation going on, they keep whispering to each other about the jockeys and the races, or the comedians and opera dancers; or about some scuffle past or future. Meantime some of them stand like statues, with their arms folded on each other; others go on blowing their noses with both hands; others sit stock still unmoved by any of my strokes of brilliancy or wit. Some try to interrupt those who do feel stirred. Others vacantly cast up the numbers in the room or stare at the trees that grow outside. But their insolence goes even beyond this. They like to hiss when others clap, or to

by Libanius, i. 199.

hinder any from applauding, or to move about across the theatre, distracting the attention of the rest, sometimes by a silly hoax, or by an invitation to an early bath . . . You know very well that this is no exaggerated grievance . . . but that the like often has occurred, and that I have often spoken out about it, and given orders that a lazy student should be taken by the collar, and thrust out of the room . . . I had a very different set of pupils once . . . Each of them used to carry something in his memory away of what I said, and then they would put their heads together and compare notes, and write my speech out fair. They were quite distressed if they lost any of the heads, although that seldom happened. For three or four days afterwards their chief employment was to go over what they knew at home before their parents, or still more in their repetitions here . . . But as for you, you forget all about Demosthenes, the latest comments as completely as the first, and go on with your songs again, which you know by heart already . . . you can only tell inquirers that I have been lecturing, but cannot repeat a word of what was said. Some one perhaps may fancy that the fault is mine, and that my lectures are not so good as they were once. Such is not the account of the older men about us; they say that they can hardly listen to my speeches quietly; they protest that I now surpass myself, that my lectures were always excellent, but that there is more in them now. You surely cannot fancy that you are better judges than they are, though you do insult them by your indifference to their excitement.'

Libanius, it will be seen, is not afraid of speaking plainly, nor of sounding his own trumpet. It may be doubted if Professors have ever scolded their pupils more freely than he did, though perhaps he had good reason, if what he says of them is true that they tried to hinder freshmen from coming to his lectures, and were overjoyed when they saw their fellow-students going off to other Universities.

There is evidence indeed that in earlier times the scholars of the Sophists were often turbulent and rude, and had to be dealt with like unruly boys. As has been already noted, it was specified as an unusual thing that in the second century, Proclus kept at Athens such strict discipline in his own circle, and would not let his pupils hiss, or play any of the pranks which, adds Philostratus, are so usual in the classes of the schoolmen. *Even in earlier ages there is like evidence of rudeness or inattention.* *Phil. ii. 106.*

Philager too was a strict martinet, for he even struck a sleepy hearer on the head when it was nodding, and once when on a visit to Herodes Atticus, he fired up because he thought a student whom he met was looking at him disrespectfully, 'What is *ii. 84.*

I

your name and country, Sir,' he asked, like a Proctor of our times, but he ended with a threat not so terrible perhaps to modern ears, 'see that you do not think of coming to any of my lectures.' 'And who are you, Sir,' was the answer, which made the Sophist still more angry, as he thought that all the world must know him. Some local vulgarism escaped him in his passion, which the student gravely noted, asking what good author he could find it in. Philager, wounded in his self-respect, sent an indignant letter to Herodes, to complain of the unseemly conduct of his pupils, who revenged themselves, however, on the hot-tempered stranger by hissing him off the scene at his first lecture, and afterwards exposing him for passing off some old speech known by heart as an extempore harangue.

Question among the Sophists as to the use of the rod.

Many of the students were mere lads, away from all control of parents, and such discipline as could be enforced among them could only come from the Professors. It was a disputed question seemingly among them whether they should rely on the influence of fear or love. Himerius, the last of the great holders of the Chair of Rhetoric at Athens, would

Himerius relies on love. xv. i 2.

only hear of the attractiveness of gentle words. He begins indeed on one occasion to rebuke plaintively the idle scholars who would not come and hear him, as foolish and ungrateful to the Master who treated them so fondly. 'Fain would I question them and say, what voice can charm your ears like mine, what gestures be so winning in your eyes, what birds of spring can sing so pleasantly as I do, what choral harmony, what blended sound of flute and pipes can touch your souls like the simple accents of this Chair. I detest those guardians of youth who cannot lead their flock, like shepherds, by the music of their pipe, but threaten them with blows and whippings. My sheep, my nurslings—may I never scare them with a frown—are to be guided by my eloquence to the groves and meadows of the Muses. To lead them I require no rod, but only melody. Music strengthens our mutual affection, and harmony gives the tone to my authority.' Such language, even from the Chair of Pastoral Theology, might be scarcely thought appropriate in these prosaic days.

Libanius did not rely so much on the persuasive power of love, and used the rod at times, we read, to say nothing of the hard words with which he freely pelted his refractory young pupils. Yet he speaks of himself in the same lecture as by far too tender hearted, as naturally prone to be patient rather than to punish. And so he shrinks from the final penalty of expulsion. 'I have friendly relations with their parents, and the cities of their birth. I fear that if they hear their sons have been expelled, they will grieve as for their death, or even more, thinking such

Libanius used the rod,

but shrunk from expulsion.
i. 207.

ignominy even worse than death, knowing that the stigma is more to be dreaded than the sentence of a court of law. The latter indeed may be reversed, but the former can never be effaced. It will cling to them from youth to age, for they may at any moment be silenced with the taunt, Shameless reprobate, were you not thrust out of the Holy Place of Learning, as defiling the temple of the Muses?'

There was something more than inattention to complain of often. <u>They did not always pay their teacher's fees, even when the money was sent them by their parents for the purpose.</u> They pressed no longer, as in olden times, to lay their fees at the Professor's feet before his chair, when the calends of January came round, while the private tutors also came with the free will offerings, which showed their love. We may hear Libanius again upon this point. 'It is enough to enrage a lecturer or make him give up teaching altogether, when the money forwarded by the father for himself is spent on wine-parties, or gambling, or immoralities still worse, and in defiance of the law.' For himself, he adds, it is no new thing for him never to be paid, and he is too much used to that to close his lecture rooms in pique, though perhaps it is no kindness to be so lenient, and they who do not pay suffer in the end, as much as the Professors who are defrauded of their fees.

Certainly to the honour of the teachers of that age

Marginalia:
Students often would not pay the fees.
Lib. i. 259.

i. 197.

be it said that they had too much enthusiastic love of their profession to think mainly of its money value. Eumenius had felt so keenly the fatal blow to learning when the schools of (Autun) Augustodunum were closed because of the ravages of war, that he was ready to forego the salary which the favour of Constantius allotted him, if it might be spent on necessary buildings for the ruined University. The speeches of the later schoolmen show that they were generous enough in remitting fees when it was needful, and helping the poorer students to get on. Themistius indeed was so liberal to the more indigent among his scholars, that some malicious gossips said he paid them to come and swell his class. 'I find,' he answers, 'recompense enough for what I do in their sense of honour, in their orderly and modest ways, in seeing that they are neither awkward, nor silly, nor ungrateful . . . None of them follows me about as if he were my servant, nor walks beside me clinging to my gown, though it is the practice of the Sophists to reap such harvests from their trade. So far indeed am I from getting any gain out of my class, that even those who call me Sophist do not dare to add that taunt, but on the contrary they say that I put up with loss, and give them food and money to stay with me, and to keep the flock together . . . Some, they say, get a mina, others two, others as much even

The Professors were often ready to forego their dues.

Paneg. Vet. Eum.

Themist. Soph.

as a talent ... Well, what of that? It seems to me more liberal and high-minded to spend my means upon my hearers, if they are in want, than to harry and torment them, or put my hand upon their throats to force the money from them, when they cannot pay.'

Many of the students were very poor. Eunap. Proær.

Many of the students seemingly were poor. Proæresius, the most famous scholar of the age, had been so poor in earlier years, that stories were repeated of his student life, to put his poverty in telling forms before the fancy. He and a fellow-student named Hephæstion, it was rumoured, only had one coat between them, and a few old dirty blankets. Only one therefore at the time could walk abroad, or go to lecture; meantime the other wrapped the bedclothes round him, and did his exercises as he could, till his turn came to wear the coat. Others like Eunapius gave private lessons to younger or less forward scholars, and so managed to pay their way and keep themselves in independence. Sometimes the richer citizens took pity on the poor students, who were living or starving near their doors, and the teachers now and then wrote letters in

Lib. Ep. 466.

such cases to appeal to the compassion of their wealthier neighbours, or to thank them for their liberal aid. There is no evidence, however, of any systematic way of helping youths of slender means.

There were no scholarship or exhibitions such as those of later times. Such endowments as existed, were confined entirely to the Professors, and the claims of studious poverty were quite ignored. *And there were no exhibitions for them.*

But at whatever sacrifice of means or comfort still they stayed on, and often found it hard to tear themselves away. Eunapius remained for a period of five years, poor as he was; Gregory was there at least for ten. The ambitious hoped to qualify themselves for teachers, setting up first as lecturers and afterwards aspiring to a Public Chair. Others, who had no such hopes or plans, and felt no spur of poverty, loved so well the Classic memories of the venerable city, and it may be also the freedom from official meddlers, that they lingered on in the old halls and only left them with regret. 'At length,' says Gregory, 'the fatal day was come, and with it all the troubles of departure; the last words of farewell, the last good wishes, the repeated leave-takings, the sighs, the tears, and the embracings. Nothing is so harrowing and so painful as for those who have been follow-students to part at last from Athens and each other. Our friends and compeers were all around us, some there were even of our tutors, protesting that they could not let us go, beseeching and imploring us to stay, and showing in everything they did or said, the evidence of genuine sorrow.' *They often remained long at the University, and left with regret.* *Greg. Naz. in laud. Basil.*

CHAPTER V.

CHRISTIAN INFLUENCES ON THE SCHOOLS OF ATHENS.

The early Sophists were free-thinkers.

THE early Sophists were the free-thinkers of old Greece. They startled the world with revolutionary maxims; they undermined the faith in the moral standards and the local institutions of each country, by appealing to a wider experience or conclusions drawn from varied data. They were the Encyclopædists of their age, the Apostles of enlightenment who set aside authority and advanced the claims of reason. The schoolmen and rhetoricians, who bore

The later were conservative in religion.

in a later age the name of Sophists, clung to the old faith, walked in the old paths, and spoke with unquestioning reverence of the Classic and the Ancient. The poetry, the art, the drama, and the history of Greece were linked so closely to the associations of religion, the fibres of Paganism had so intertwined themselves round all that they held dear, that when the final struggle came at last, they rallied as volunteers in a forlorn hope, for the defence of the Hellenic creed, whose theologians had been Hesiod

and Homer. 'For,' says Libanius, 'religion and cul- ii'. 43.
ture are close friends, or even near of kin, both for
Philosophers and Sophists, and for all who are initi-
ated into the rites of Hermes and the Muses.'

Some things there were perhaps in the old poems,
which, written as they had been for a people's child-
hood, were scarcely suited for robuster thought;
passages too gross and sensual not to shock at times a
reverent fancy; but there were canons of interpreta-
tion ready, which found an allegory in each romance,
resolved persons and places into mere abstractions, and
shifted the reasoner at will into the realms of trans-
cendental dreamland. The philosophers took kindly as were
the philo-
to these principles of Hermeneutic, and on the basis sophers of
later days,
of this new concordat enrolled themselves in the Eunap.
service of Religion, and were of all men most devout. Chrysan.
Thus one of whom Eunapius tells us was a High
Priest of Lydia, another lived in the temples to a
great old age, and others are spoken of as busy with
sacrifice and divination, and as staunch defenders of
the faith.

So familiar were they with the unseen and who often
claimed
supernatural, that they often claimed and were mysterious
powers over
believed to have a mysterious hold upon the spirit the spirit
world.
world, and the writer just referred to tells us strange
tales of power to foresee the far-off both in time and
space, and to make unearthly beings answer to their

call. It is no wonder if the Christians took them at their word, and believed that they were leagued with powers of darkness; their religion seemed but an unclean demon-worship, its ritual only sorcery or magic. And so the cry grew louder to sweep away the accursed thing, and Christian Emperors soon began to discourage if not to suppress the older faith.

The Christians took them at their word and tried to put them down.

Thus Eunapius thinks that possibly Ædesius concealed his gift of inspiration, because of the hard times. 'For Constantine then reigned, who threw down the most famous temples, and raised Christian Churches in their stead. Whence it came to pass that the wisest philosophers took refuge in mysterious silence and reserve becoming to their priestly office. So much so that the writer of these lives, though a pupil of Chrysanthius, was scarce thought worthy of admission to the truth until his twentieth year, so hard a matter was it for the doctrines of Iamblichus to be introduced and gradually spread among us, for after he was taken from us the men of note were scattered here and there, and none were left of any worth or reputation.'

Eunap. Ædes.

The same discouragement was felt ere long, though to a less extent perhaps, by the schools of rhetoric and the Sophists. Christians still flocked indeed to Athens, where the Pagan sentiment was intensely strong, and where all the greater schoolmen known, save

The disfavour was extended from the philosophers to the schools of rhetoric.

Proæresius, still clung to the older faith of Hellas. But the language of Gregory implies that the feelings of fear and antipathy were strong in pious minds, for men, he says 'are more prone there to idol worship than in all the rest of Greece, and it is not easy to avoid being carried into error in the company of those who are its champions and panegyrists.' He is thankful that he did not suffer from these spiritual dangers, which were fatal, as he owns, to others; but his friend Basil found the spirit of the place so uncongenial, that he was not easily induced to stay where there was much that seemed to him so vain and worldly. Greg. Naz. in laud. Basil.

Yet before long Libanius complained that the Imperial Court looked with an evil eye upon the Schools, and that the malign influence was spreading fast. An enemy had taunted him with his failure as a teacher, and asked how many of his scholars had risen in the world. In his reply the orator dilates upon the unfriendly bearing of the Christian rulers. Constantius never summoned them to Court, or said a kindly word, or heard them lecture; but allowed a wretched set of barbarous eunuchs to govern in his name, and they conspired to drive away the men of education, and promote the enemies of heaven and starveling upstarts to the posts of honour. The students naturally asked, what is the use of all our The complaints of Libanius of the discouragement felt by students. iii. 486.

reading if it will not raise us in the world. Parents preferred to put their sons to Law, and sent them to the University of Berytus, as literary skill was prized so little. Even after spending years among the Schools of Athens, where philosophy and rhetoric had engaged their thoughts, men were glad to take a place as Emperor's messenger, or to wear the livery of his household servants. If such discouragements were felt at Athens, still more were they to be feared in places near the Court, where all its sympathies were fully known. He owns indeed that a transient gleam of sunshine rested on the fortunes of the Schools when they enjoyed a period of Royal favour.

Brighter times came in with Julian's accession to the throne.

Julian, the so-called Apostate, had wearied early of his pious exercises with the Christian priests, and pored by stealth over the lectures of Libanius. Allowed at length to come to Athens, he drank deeply at the sources of the old Hellenic culture, and long before he dropped the mask, had lost, if indeed he ever had, affection for the faith which was full to his mind of memories of controversial quibbles and of harsh constraint. One of his first acts when he claimed the sovereign power was to send his manifesto to the old seat of learning, to show that he was not a vulgar adventurer prompted by ambition, but a scholar who could do justice to the goodness of his cause, and deserve the sympathy of the world of letters.

The Sages and the Sophists gladly welcomed the young prince, whose sumpter mules were laden, not with costly furniture and viands, but with a precious freight of books. They hailed the dawn of a new era when philosophy had once more mounted on the throne, and another Antonine was ready with enlightened patronage of men of worth. The new ruler was not slow to do his part. Libanius, whom he so much admired in earlier years, was treated by him with a cordial respect; honours were showered on the graver thinkers, the theologians of the philosophic creed which he espoused; the greatest of them, whom Eunapius mentions, were invited to his Court, and kept ever in his company to while away the tedium of the Persian campaign.

<small>Lib. iii. 440.</small>

<small>who showed special favour to the Sophists,</small>

Prompted or encouraged by their councils, he forgot his usual toleration, and denied the Christians leave to teach in the schools of rhetoric and liberal study, affecting to regard them as mere ignorant fanatics, sworn foes of all the older culture, iconoclasts in arts and letters. One only of the Athenian Professors, the celebrated Proæresius, was exempted from this penal clause, but he was too generous to stand alone, and though he probably had little in him of the martyr's stuff, forbore to lecture when his friends were silenced.

<small>but denied Christians leave to teach in the schools.</small>

For a few short months the schoolmen's pent-up

bitterness found vent, and they triumphed as if their rivals' downfall were complete. But wiser eyes had seen already that the adverse currents were too strong, and the reaction could not last. Thus Chrysanthius of Lydia, when sent for to the Court, whether warned by mysterious portents, as Eunapius believed, or possibly by natural insight, declined all the brilliant offers made by Julian, answering like Balaam, that his God refused him leave to come. 'Thereupon the Emperor wrote to him again, and sent letters not to himself only, but to his wife, that haply she might influence her husband. A second time Chrysanthius had recourse to divination, but again no favouring signs appeared. This happened several times, for still the Emperor was earnest in his wish to see him.' He read the future clearly, though he could not have foreseen that Julian's death was sadly near, and with it the funeral knell of the last hopes of Pagan Greece.

Athens found ere long that the privilege of Imperial favour had been a source of weakness rather than of strength. It had made men feel how intensely anti-christian was the spirit of her schools, and how great was the possible danger of a like revival. First came the legal prohibition, in the name of Valens, against any magic sacrifice or rites, and terms so vague and so elastic might be stretched to cover any

The triumph of the Sophists was short-lived,

Eunap. Chrysan- as the wiser of them foresaw.

The death of Julian was followed by edicts against Paganism, of the forms of divination, any of the mysteries of theurgy, in which the later systems of philosophy abounded. Two of the favourites of Julian suffered probably on this account, though Eunapius tells us only of their imprisonment and pains, and is silent as to the exact nature of the charges. Others withdrew themselves from public sight, and, in the words of their biographer, 'grieved themselves to early death.' Priscus Maximus.

They might save themselves from actual danger, but they could not screen from desecration all that they held dear. Bands of rioters broke loose, encouraged by their spiritual heads, while the civil power quietly stood by and made no sign. The temples were destroyed, the shrines defiled. How sorely the blow was felt by pious minds we may gather from the language of Eunapius, when he speaks of the governors of Egypt who levelled the great temple of Serapis to the ground, and carried all away save the foundations, which were too massive for them to remove. 'Thus these warlike and courageous champions, after causing general ruin, and stretching forth their hands, not stained with blood indeed, but befouled with avarice, boasted that they had overcome the Gods, and taking credit for their impiety and sacrilege, let loose against the holy places the so-called monks, who were men indeed in outward shape, but of swinish life and manners, who openly committed abominations without number. They thought it an act of piety to spurn reverence for the Divine. For anyone who liked to put a black coat upon his back, and a sour look upon his face, could lord it like a tyrant. . . . So they settled these monks about Canopus, and degraded men to worship slaves and reprobates instead of the Gods of a reasonable service. For they gathered up the heads of those who had been put to death as malefactors for their many crimes, and pointed to them as their Gods, and rolled themselves in the dirt beside their tombs. At least they called them martyrs, and ministers or ambassadors in their prayers to Heaven, though they were but sorry slaves and whipping-stocks, who carried on their bodies the scars of blows which they had richly merited.'

and Libanius. ii. 164. Libanius also, in another country, vents his indignation in no measured terms. 'This black-coated gentry, who are more ravenous than elephants, and drink so often as to weary out the patience of the congregations who have to chaunt meantime at every draught, though they disguise their habits by the artificial pallor of their faces—these in defiance of existing laws hurry to attack the temples, some with staves and stones and steel, others even with fisticuffs and kicks. They fall an easy prey, the roofs are stripped, the is hurled down, the statues dragged away, the altars overthrown. The priests must hold their peace or die. When one is ruined they hurry to a second or a third, and pile fresh trophies in defiance of the law. Such acts of daring occur even in the cities, but far more in the country. ... So they sweep like winter-torrents through the land, making havoc of it for the temples' sake.' He goes on to describe the consternation of the country folks, robbed of the objects of their reverence, and of all their hopes of divine favour and protection. 'If the poor wretches thus despoiled betake themselves with their complaints to the pastor in the city,—for pastor they call some worthless guide,—he only praises the ill-doers, and drives away the sufferers with the taunt that they are lucky in not having been treated even worse. ... Yet they are the working bees who suffer, while the others are the drones.'

These blows were fatal, not to the temples only, but also to the schools of ..., which were linked so closely to the associations of religion. Two other influences also largely tended to complete their downfall. One was the ascendancy which legal studies now were gaining, and the consequent attraction of the Universities of Rome and Berytus, in which they mainly flourished. Libanius often vents his spleen at such unbecoming rivalry. 'In old days,' he says, 'the experts in the law stood in court

The schools of Athens suffered from the downfall of Paganism, as also from the greater popularity of legal and Latin studies.

humbly looking to the orator, and waiting till he said "read the clauses for me;" now even the scriveners fill the highest posts.' Still more potent was the change of fashion by which the Roman tongue and Roman letters were brought once more into special favour. Even the influence of the court at Constantinople was used in that direction, and Latin was still the language of the ruling powers. The same writer tells us of his fears that his favourite studies would be soon suppressed by law; and though this indeed was not the case, yet they had been effectually degraded by the prizes and encouragements awarded to their rival. Soon the Greek Church, which he thought his most formidable foe, would have to gather what was falling from the Sophists' hands, and preserve the heritage of the old Hellenic culture.

The complaints become more numerous as time goes on; the schools of rhetoric are fast declining, and the schoolmen's trade is nearly gone. For a few years, in the case of Athens, the 'magni nominis umbra' powerfully affects the imagination of the learned, and towards the close even of the fourth century Synesius satirically notes the airs assumed by those who had made a pilgrimage to the old city. 'They are only mortals after all, and like ourselves; they do not understand Plato or Aristotle better than we do, yet they think of themselves as demigods among a set of mules, so proud are they of having looked on the Academy and Lyceum, and the Porch where Zenon reasoned.' He came, indeed, himself to Athens, but only to be more convinced that such a pilgrimage was idle folly. 'There is nothing here of note,' he wrote, 'except the local names which are renowned. As the skin of the beast that has been killed and eaten is the sign of its past life, so now that philosophy is dead and gone there is nothing left for me but to roam about and gaze with curious eyes on the Academy, the Lyceum, and the painted Porch, which gave its name to the system of Chrysippus, but which is no more painted, now that the Governor has carried off the pictures, in which the Thasian Polygnotus stored his art. In our own days Egypt fosters the germs of life, which she has gathered from Hypatia. Athens was once the home of sages; now-a-days its only credit comes from the keepers of its beehives. So is it with the learned pair of Plutarch's school, who win their youthful hearers, not by the reputation of their lectures, but by the attractions of the wine-jars of Hyméttus.'

Ep. 136.

but he speaks with contempt of the studies carried on there.

 Yet to the fancy of the pious Pagans the powers of Heaven still watched with favouring care over the old city which had worshipped them so fondly and so long. In the earthquake which shook all Greece, in

To pious eyes heaven still seemed to watch over the city;

the reign of Valens, Athens alone escaped by special grace, if Zosimus be trusted. A still more marked deliverance is recorded by the same historian, when Alaric led his northmen to the south, and swept over the undefended country. He made his way through the narrow passage of Thermopylæ, betrayed to him by the governor Gerontius, or, as Eunapius will have it, by the monks, and appeared before the walls of Athens, which were likely to fall an easy prey. But Providence then stayed his hand by marvellous portents. He saw Athena, the tutelary goddess, walking in armour on the walls, as if ready to beat off assailants. 'He saw Achilles in heroic posture, as Homer showed him to the Trojans when he fought against them so furiously to avenge the slaughter of Patroclus.' So Alaric forbore to press the siege, and offered favourable terms; and, thanks to the protection of the gods, Athens escaped almost unscathed. However that might be, we hear no more of schools of rhetoric and Sophists at the ancient University; the studious youth repaired to it no longer, though a few philosophers, driven perhaps from Alexandria by religious riots, sought for awhile a haven of refuge in the quiet scenes that once were thronged with strangers.

They were members of that school of Plutarch which Synesius spoke of mockingly, though, Christian as he was, he had much in common with the Neoplatonic speculations. The last survivor of the systems, which, born of the Socratic thought, had gone out into the world to seek their fortunes, it made its way back to the old home to die. It lingered on a century or more with few adherents, and with little stir, devoting all its industry and erudition to the effort to harmonise the leading principles of the great historic systems, and reconcile the claims of faith and reason in a vast scheme of theosophy to which Greece supplied the method, while the inspiration was borrowed from the East.

At last came the fatal edict of Justinian, which forbade anyone to teach philosophy, or expound the law, at Athens. *(Till the edict of Justinian led to their departure. A.D. 529.)*

Nor was this all. Procopius, a contemporary writer, speaks of the sweeping measure by which the Emperor withheld all the grants of public money made by former rulers to the interests of learning, and goes on to accuse him even of confiscating all the endowments for like objects, due to the liberality of private citizens in view of the common weal. This probably included in its range the little revenues of the Socratic schools, which were at once reduced to poverty and silence.

'So seven sages,' as Agathias tells us, 'the flower of the philosophy of those times, abandoned at once *(ii. 30.)*

the Roman world, where, by reason of the recent edicts, they could no longer enjoy their civil freedom save by compliance with the established faith. They resolved to live under the rule of Persia, which they thought, like others of their day, to be a Platonic union of philosophy and kingly power, while the people were temperate and just. But they found things far other than they hoped. There were the old familiar vices, or even worse, in common life: arrogance among the nobles; and in the Monarch Chosroes, notwithstanding some slight hankering for philosophy a total want of higher culture, and a bigoted adherence to the national customs. They soon became home-sick again, though Chosroes liked them and much wished them to remain.'

They gained at least something by their visit, for in the treaty made between the Persian and the Roman empires favourable terms were introduced to enable such of the philosophers as chose to return in safety and live undisturbed. Damascius and Simplicius at least went back, not indeed to teach in public, but to cling as before to the old Hellenic rites, and possibly to enjoy a few years longer the endowments of their school.

They betook themselves to Persia,

but only to be disappointed of their hopes.

Spottiswoode & Co., Printers, New-street Square, London.

www.ingramcontent.com/pod-product-compliance
Lightning Source LLC
Chambersburg PA
CBHW030358170426
43202CB00010B/1410